getting
RESULTS

instant manager
skills for success

getting
RESULTS

BERNICE WALMSLEY

HODDER
EDUCATION
PART OF HACHETTE LIVRE UK

Orders: Please contact Bookpoint Ltd, 130 Milton Park, Abingdon, Oxon OX14 4SB. Telephone: (44) 01235 827720, Fax: (44) 01235 400454. Lines are open from 9.00 to 5.00, Monday to Saturday, with a 24-hour message answering service. You can also order through our website www.hoddereducation.co.uk.

British Library Cataloguing in Publication Data
A catalogue record for this title is available from the British Library.

ISBN-13: 978 0340 94735 7

First published   2009
Impression number   10 9 8 7 6 5 4 3 2 1
Year   2012 2011 2010 2009

Typeset by Transet Limited, Coventry, England.
Printed in Great Britain for Hodder Education, an Hachette Livre UK Company, 338 Euston Road, London NW1 3BH, by Cox & Wyman, Reading, Berkshire RG1 8EX.

Hachette Livre UK's policy is to use papers that are natural, renewable and recyclable products and made from wood grown in sustainable forests. The logging and manufacturing processes are expected to conform to the environmental regulations of the country of origin.

The Chartered Management Institute

The Chartered Management Institute is the only chartered professional body that is dedicated to management and leadership. We are committed to raising the performance of business by championing management.

We represent 80,000 individual managers and have 450 corporate members. Within the Institute there are also a number of distinct specialisms, including the Institute of Business Consulting and Women in Management Network.

We exist to help managers tackle the management challenges they face on a daily basis by raising the standard of management in the UK. We are here to help individuals become better managers and companies develop better managers.

We do this through a wide range of products and services, from practical management checklists to tailored training and qualifications. We produce research on the latest 'hot' management issues, provide a vast array of useful information through our online management information centre, as well as offering consultancy services and career information.

You can access these resources 'off the shelf' or we can provide solutions just for you. Our range of products and services is designed to ensure organisations and managers develop their potential and excel. Whether you are at the start of your career or a proven performer in the boardroom, we have something for you.

We engage policy makers and opinion formers and, as the leading authority on management, we are regularly consulted on a range of management issues. Through our in-depth research and regular policy surveys of members, we have a deep understanding of the latest management trends.

For more information visit our website **www.managers.org.uk** or call us on **01536 207307**.

Chartered Manager

Transform the way you work

The Chartered Management Institute's Chartered Manager award is the ultimate accolade for practising professional managers. Designed to transform the way you think about your work and how you add value to your organisation, it is based on demonstrating measurable impact.

This unique award proves your ability to make a real difference in the workplace.

Chartered Manager focuses on the six vital business skills of:

- Leading people
- Managing change
- Meeting customer needs
- Managing information and knowledge
- Managing activities and resources
- Managing yourself

Transform your organisation

There is a clear and well-established link between good management and improved organisational performance. Recognising this, the Chartered Manager scheme requires individuals to demonstrate how they are applying their leadership and change management skills to make significant impact within their organisation.

Transform your career

Whatever career stage a manager is at Chartered Manager will set them apart. Chartered Manager has proven to be a stimulus to career progression, either via recognition by their current employer or through the motivation to move on to more challenging roles with new employers.

But don't take just our word for it ...

Chartered Manager has transformed the careers and organisations of managers in all sectors.

- *'Being a Chartered Manager was one of the main contributing factors which led to my recent promotion.'*
  Lloyd Ross, Programme Delivery Manager, British Nuclear Fuels

- *'I am quite sure that a part of the reason for my success in achieving my appointment was due to my Chartered Manager award which provided excellent, independent evidence that I was a high quality manager.'*
  Donaree Marshall, Head of Programme Management Office, Water Service, Belfast

- *'The whole process has been very positive, giving me confidence in my strengths as a manager but also helping me to identify the areas of my skills that I want to develop. I am delighted and proud to have the accolade of Chartered Manager.'*
  Allen Hudson, School Support Services Manager, Dudley Metropolitan County Council

- *'As we are in a time of profound change, I believe that I have, as a result of my change management skills, been able to provide leadership to my staff. Indeed, I took over three teams and carefully built an integrated team, which is beginning to perform really well. I believe that the process I went through to gain Chartered Manager status assisted me in achieving this and consequently was of considerable benefit to my organisation.'*
  George Smart, SPO and D/Head of Resettlement, HM Prison Swaleside

To find out more or to request further information please visit our website **www.managers.org.uk/cmgr** or call us on **01536 207429**.

Contents

CHAPTER 05

CHAPTER 06

CHAPTER 07

CHAPTER 08

CHAPTER 09

CHAPTER 10

Foreword

There has never been a greater need for better management and leadership skills in the UK. As we've seen over the past couple of years, it's all too often the case that management incompetence takes the blame for high-profile, costly and sometimes tragic failures. Put this in the context of a world dominated by changing technology and growing international competition, and every manager in this country has a responsibility for ensuring that he or she has the best possible skills to contribute to successful business performance.

So it is alarming that just one in five managers in the UK are professionally qualified. The truth is that we spend less on management development in the UK than our European competitors. Effectively this means that, if you want to develop professionally, if you want to boost your career chances, or if you just want recognition for the work you do, the onus is on you – the individual – to improve your skills. What it also means is that all of us – individual managers, employers and policy makers – need to answer difficult questions about how well equipped we are to lead in the 21st century. Are our standards slipping? How capable are we when it comes to meeting the skill requirements of modern business? Studies show that project management, alliance-building and communication skills are the three key 'over-arching' skills that must be mastered by the successful manager. But how many people can honestly claim they have mastery over all three?

In recent years the news has been dominated by stories focusing on breathtaking management failures. The collapse of the banking sector has been much-analysed and will continue to be discussed in the years to come. It's not just the private sector. Vast amounts of column inches have been devoted to investigations of failures across the health and social care services, too. The spotlight has also been on management, at an individual level, as the recession has deepened in the aftermath of the banking crisis, with dramatic rises in the UK's unemployment levels. Many managers are fighting an ongoing battle to control costs and survive with reduced credit and slowing demand. They are also struggling to prove their worth, to show they meet required standards now, and in the long-term.

But imagine a world where management and leadership enables top-class performance right across British businesses, the public sector and our not-for-profit organisations – where management isn't a byword for bureaucracy and failure, but plays a real role in boosting performance. The way to achieve such a realistic utopia is by developing the skills that will help you, as a manager, perform to the best of your capability. And that is why this book will help. Its aim is to provide you with practical, digestible advice that you can take straight from the pages to apply in your working environment.

Does any of this matter? Well, you wouldn't want your accounts signed off by someone lacking a financial qualification. You certainly wouldn't let an unqualified surgeon anywhere near you with a scalpel, nor would you seek an unqualified lawyer to represent your interests. Why, then, should your employer settle for management capability that is second best? It means that you need to take time out to develop your skills so that these can be evaluated and so you can stand out from the competition.

What's more, managers will play a critical role in determining how well the UK meets a wide range of challenges over the next decade. How can managers foster innovation to promote economic growth? How do they tackle the gender pay gap and the continued under-representation of women in the boardroom, as part of building truly fair, diverse organisations? Managers in all sectors will need to learn how to lead their teams through the changes we face; they will also need to be able to manage change. Above all, managers will need to grasp the nettle when it comes to managing information and knowledge. The key will rest in how they learn to manage themselves.

First-class management and leadership really can drive up both personal and corporate performance. It can boost national productivity and enhance social wellbeing. If you want to be the best manager you can be, this book is for you. In one go it will provide you with practical advice and the experience of business leaders. It is also a fascinating and enthralling read!

Ruth Spellman OBE
Chief Executive
Chartered Management Institute

Acknowledgements

Thanks must go, as ever, to my husband William for his support, patience and encouragement and to Andrew Hill of Committed Network for his help with the Gantt chart.

Grateful thanks also to Alison Frecknall and the team at Hodder for all their friendly help and guidance during the commissioning and production of this book.

Introduction

Who should read this book?

If you want to upgrade your management skills, then this series of books – a sub-strand of the Instant Manager series – is for you. The series covers a range of skills essential for today's manager and deals with those set out in the employer-led set of standards (the National Occupational Standards) for leadership and management. These were drawn up to improve the productivity and profitability of organisations in the UK, as well as helping with career development, so are of benefit to employees and employers alike.

This book is for any manager – new or experienced – who needs help with achieving results in their working life. It is not jargon-filled or too complicated and theory-bound. It contains practical advice to help you in your working life. So, if you need to acquire the knowledge needed to get results, to understand the marketing element of your job and also to be able to deal with customer service in a competent and knowledgeable manner, then this book is for you.

A range of topics, linked by the common themes of improving performance in your organisation and enhancing your own skills set, is covered by each book in the series in the form of ten questions. In this book you will find the answers to questions that will show you how to manage the various aspects of customer service, including resolving customer complaints and improving customer service, and also how to deal with quality standards and some aspects of marketing.

At the end of each chapter, after a specific question has been answered, there will be a summary of what has been discussed, and a short action checklist, which gives you the series of practical steps you need to take to overcome the challenge of that topic at work.

The skills that you will learn in this book are vital to your success as a manager. Of course, the skills you need are many and varied, so in this book we will be concentrating on the ones that are vital to ensuring you meet customer needs and get results.

What skills do you need to get results?

Many of the skills necessary to get results in a customer-focused environment are those that all managers need. After all, all managers need to deal with customers of some kind or to improve performance. But there are also specific skills that will be vital if you are to arrive at a successful outcome and meet the targets that have been set for you in your job – or which you have set for yourself.

General management skills, such as delegation and communication, will be useful in ensuring your team know what is required of them, and more specific ones such as problem solving and planning will be vital in, for example, developing a customer service strategy.

Let's look in a little more detail at the main areas we need to consider when we want to achieve results:

- **Marketing** – when you become involved in marketing for your organisation it is important that you are able to think strategically. You will need to place customers at the centre of all of the things that you do in this area so you will need to understand just who your customers are and to think creatively about how you will satisfy their requirements. In marketing there is always a lot of data to deal with, so being able to manage information and to evaluate that data will be vital skills.
- **Customer service** – this is a particularly important area to the competitiveness of any organisation and requires a variety of skills, not least of which are communication and negotiation. For example, you will need to identify customer service problems and for this you will have to communicate carefully with customers. To do this you will need well-developed listening skills as well as the ability to convey what you will do to help. Subsequently you will have to resolve the problem and, in order to avoid the repetition of similar problems, will need to monitor and analyse the issue, then put in place measures to improve your organisation's customer service.
- **Quality** – dealing with the legal and regulatory requirements imposed on organisations by formal quality management systems requires a variety of skills including an attention to detail and the ability to present information. Analytical skills will help when dealing with the corrective action that may be necessary after a quality audit.

- **Sales** – in any sales environment the skills involved in communication (both written and spoken) will be of paramount importance. However, others such as analytical skills, and a thorough knowledge of the organisation's capabilities, products and services, are also vital.

After that brief overview, let's move on to the first of our questions. This looks at two areas – projects and processes – that you will need to be able to understand and manage to ensure you get results.

02

How can you manage processes and projects to get results?

Managing processes and projects is something that all managers do as part of their responsibilities. There are also full-time project managers who will not only follow the principles of managing projects to deliver a project on budget and on time, as outlined in this chapter, but will also use one or more project management tools. This is a specialised subject area and, as such, is outside the scope of this book. However, in this book we hope to give you the basic tools to tackle a project as required in any manager's role. If your work role involves a significant element of large project management, then more detailed information can be obtained from books and organisations listed in the 'Further information and reading' section at the end of this book.

Before we can manage either processes or projects to get results, we must first understand the difference between them. A process is an activity that takes place continuously in an organisation or in a familiar sequence repeated when necessary. Projects are separate from processes. Projects are set up to develop and improve processes and also to develop new products. Projects are a sequence of tasks that are performed in order to reach a unique goal. They are usually done just once, whereas processes are carried out frequently.

Defining business processes

The ability to define the processes at work in our own organisation is essential if we are to undertake projects to improve them. Let's look at how processes and projects work together in an example situation.

A call centre worker taking a telephone call will follow a sequence of actions for every phone call – this is a process. There might be minor variations in how he or she handles the call – the caller may be irate or confused for example – but this will have happened often enough for the operative to have established a sequence of actions appropriate for such occasions. However, there may be some changes that are more serious and need additional actions working out so that the operative can deal with them. The call centre could, for example, take on the work of fielding calls for a large multinational company and occasionally receive calls from non-English speakers. In this instance, a small project may be necessary to establish a new set of actions. The project may well decide that a team of translators or interpreters should be put in place and a new set of actions set up so that the operative who is faced with a non-English speaking caller knows exactly how to transfer the call to the appropriate translator. So, in essence, a process is a set of actions whereas a project is used to solve a problem by changing a sequence of actions or setting up a new sequence of actions.

A more comprehensive definition of a business process is that it is a sequence of linked procedures that are interdependent and that consume resources (time, money, labour) in order to convert inputs into outputs. This definition shows how managing processes must be an integral part of any manager's role. A manager must manage these processes, continually reviewing and improving them. Business Process Management (BPM) is, like project management in its more complicated form, worthy of far greater detail than is possible in this book. For more information see the 'Further information and reading' section. However, we will set out the basics here with a more general approach.

Managing business processes

Process improvement can be carried out in three main stages:

1. First by defining an organisation's purpose and objectives. Here questions such as, 'Who are we?', 'What do we do?' and, 'Where are we going?' should be asked and answered.
2. Describing the organisation's customers – there is more detail on this in Chapter 3 – and finding out how the organisation's processes affect these customers.
3. Aligning the organisation's business processes so that they achieve its goals. This should answer the question, 'How can we do it better?'

In order to be able to improve business processes it is important to define the ones in operation in your department and evaluate their performance. A useful way of evaluating a process is to conduct a cost–benefit analysis. This compares how well or how badly a process is going by quantifying all the negative aspects (the costs) and deducting them from the total of the positive aspects (the benefits). If the benefits outweigh the costs then the process is working. If this exercise is carried out regularly on the major processes in your area of responsibility, it will show whether or not improvements are being made. It should also be used to see if a change to current processes is worth making. It is important that all costs and benefits are included in this analysis. Frequently, managers concentrate on the benefits possible from a proposed action and gloss over the costs, missing out some less obvious, but still significant, costs.

There are many tools that can be used to facilitate Business Process Improvement, many of them software-based. Simple measures, such as the use of flowcharts to illustrate processes, can be useful. Also, as it is closely aligned to quality management, systems and standards such as Total Quality Management (TQM) and ISO 9000 can be used. Similarly, in manufacturing, techniques such as Just in Time (JIT) or Lean Manufacturing will be used.

It is possible to start Business Process Improvement on a small scale by choosing a small process that can easily be defined and that will result in a short exercise in its improvement within well-defined time frames. A small process will attract less opposition internally and will be easier to manage. However, like all projects, Business Process Improvements require the usual inputs to ensure success:

- excellent leadership and support
- planning
- an acknowledgement of the need to change
- adequate resources
- all-encompassing communication
- careful implementation
- thorough evaluation.

An important aspect of managing a project is preparing a comprehensive description of the processes involved in the project. Unless all the processes are fully understood, the project will not succeed, so we will look next at managing projects.

Key management challenges in managing a project

Projects have to be seen to show results. They have to produce recognisable and measurable business benefits. Delivering those results – on time, on budget and to an acceptable quality threshold – is always the main challenge for anyone who has to manage a project. Project management is a huge topic but one which many managers have to get to grips with early on in their careers. Even if you are not called upon to manage a project, your job will undoubtedly be affected by them at some point.

So, what is a project?

- A project will produce a change in one or more processes carried out in an organisation.
- It has a defined beginning and end, so a specific project should not be an indefinite part of your work role.
- It is planned and controlled.
- It has defined objectives.
- It must produce measurable benefits.
- It has allocated resources.

There are a number of well-documented approaches to project management and it is not possible to detail all, or even a few, of these methods in this book. What we will give here is an overview of project stages and how to cope with the challenges that managing a project will bring.

Projects come in all shapes and sizes – they can be small and straightforward or they can be wide-ranging and complex. They all need managing, but the management of larger projects will inevitably be more complex than that of small ones. If you have a complex project to manage you will probably use a standard project management method such as PRINCE2™ and extensive training will be necessary, but again this type of method is outside the scope of this book.

First you will need to pick your team. This may need very little input from you on small projects, but extensive involvement of the project manager is essential in the case of large, wide-ranging projects that will have a long life. It is essential that you ensure that the team includes a wide variety of skills and disciplines. As we said previously, projects are results driven so you will need to ensure that all members of your team have a good understanding of the objectives of the project and how they are going to achieve them.

Having chosen your team, it is a good idea to involve them in the planning stage itself as this will not only ensure that the planning is carried out by people with a variety of skills and viewpoints, but also you will be able to gain the support, agreement and commitment of your team during this early stage in the project.

As we've already said, the main challenge in managing a project is in delivering the required results on time and on budget. Along the way there will undoubtedly be many other challenges. One of these will probably be for the people involved to keep a sense of proportion about the project. It can be difficult for someone managing or closely involved with a project to keep a work–life balance. The project and its aims can become all-consuming. Good planning and a clear vision of what you are trying to achieve – and why – will help with this. Being able to adapt to circumstances will also be an invaluable skill when working on projects as barriers, changes and unexpected developments are an inevitable feature of all projects. Being able to recognise changes, deal with the unexpected and to overcome barriers is vital. Comprehensive planning and continually reviewing the progress of the project will ensure that problems are recognised and dealt with before too much harm is done to either the project or the organisation as a whole. Keeping the project on track is the main thing to focus on, so continual reference to the plan is needed.

Regardless of the approach to project management that is used, a project will go through several recognised stages:

- initiation
- planning
- implementation
- monitoring
- closing.

The next few sections will look at these stages one by one.

Sorting out your priorities – setting key objectives

When an organisation detects problems, a project will often be put in place to solve a perceived problem, but it is vital that a project is not undertaken lightly and without due consideration and planning. Change is a risk and it would be unwise to go into a business-changing project without analysing the business and being satisfied that the project is worthwhile and will solve the problem.

It is at this initiation stage that the scope of the project is decided. A lot of research and decision making goes on at this point and it is vital to the success of the project that this is done thoroughly and with all the necessary information to hand. The first priority must be to establish an understanding of the business needs and the environment in which it is working. All the business processes involved in the area of the project should be analysed. At this point the goals of the project will be set and all the other project parameters, such as the projected costs and the resources that will be available, must be decided upon. The project's viability and the returns expected from the project must be clear to enable the project's sponsors and the financial managers to decide whether or not the project should go ahead.

In view of the possible amount of time and other resources that could be wasted by continuing with a project that is unlikely to succeed, a number of checks should be carried out before going on to the next stage:

1. Are the objectives of the project completely clear?
2. Are the necessary resources available? This includes time on the part of the person managing the project and the staff to ensure it can be carried out effectively.
3. Have you got a sufficiently detailed description of the project in writing? This should preferably be done by the project's sponsor so that you are fully aware of his or her vision of what the outcomes will be.
4. Are the outcomes agreed by all – including you as project manager, the financial management of the organisation and all stakeholders in the project?
5. Do you understand how the proposed project fits into the organisation's vision and objectives?
6. Do you have all the relevant facts to hand?

At the end of the Initiation Stage the terms of reference of the project can be set out in a statement. This should include:

- the exact scope of the project
- why the project is being undertaken
- the roles and responsibilities of all the main players
- the outcomes, along with a detailed timescale for achieving them.

These terms of reference provide a document that is useful in a variety of ways including:

- as a sales document for the project so that stakeholders can decide whether or not to give the go-ahead based on the returns expected and the scope of the project
- as a guide for the project – a useful reference point throughout the project's life to remind everyone concerned what has been agreed
- as authorisation for the project.

When you are satisfied that you have all the necessary authorisations, information and resources in place then you can proceed to the next stage – Planning.

Make a plan

Having decided where you are going – the objectives for the project – you will now need to decide how you are going to get there – the plan. You must be clear about the project's objectives, its context and constraints, and the resources that will be available for you to achieve it. It is also helpful to clarify just how the project will be judged. You should be clear about how you will prove that you have satisfied any user requirements that you have identified at this stage.

INSTANT TIP

Remember, successful project management is not simply about delivering results – it is about delivering the right results and also showing that you have done so.

When you have reached this level of understanding, you can then begin to prepare a work breakdown structure. To prepare this you will need to include the following:

- a list all the activities of the project in manageable parts
- how long each activity is expected to take
- estimate of costs
- control of costs
- agreed outcomes
- linked activities.

Care must be taken when considering the level of detail to include in a work breakdown schedule. This schedule is not intended to be used as a set of instructions on how to carry out the work as this would limit the project severely. It is a list of the work elements of a project showing the links between each element. Each element should be a distinct package of work that could be outsourced if required, or allocated to a member (or members) of the project team. So long as it is clear what the package of work is meant to achieve, it is not necessary to go into greater detail about the tasks included in the package. In effect this stage of the planning procedure is the design stage – the exact timings of each of the work elements must come later. The main priority at this stage is to get all the work that has to be accomplished down on paper in the right level of detail.

After the work breakdown schedule has been established and agreed, further planning can take place. A particularly useful tool at the planning stage and throughout the life of the project is a Gantt chart. This is a type of bar chart that shows, in graphic form, the different stages of the project. It illustrates the start and finish dates of each element of the project and can be used during the project to show the progress that has been made by using percentage shading of each element to show how much has been completed and also by the addition of a 'today' line that will highlight the point that the project has reached. A Gantt chart will also show which parts of the project overlap. It is important that this type of planning tool is used after the work breakdown structure has been prepared – it can cause unnecessary confusion and possible omissions if you attempt to prepare both the work breakdown and the Gantt chart at the same time. Gantt charts can be prepared using easily available software. Look at the example shown in Figure 2.1 on page 16.

A Gantt chart is usually prepared by entering detail from the work breakdown schedule into the relevant software package. One thing to take particular care about is the dependency and timing of the various work elements. It is tempting to try to shorten the project by allowing a second stage to commence before another is completed, when in reality it relies on results from this preceding stage. Remember that what you produce on a complicated-looking chart will not change reality. The work still has to be done and it will be done a great deal more efficiently if this planning stage is completed honestly, realistically and comprehensively.

Implementation

It is at this stage that systems are put into place that will allow the project to take place and the project manager to control the risks, outcomes and resources. The only way to ensure that the project remains on track is to refer back constantly to the planning. It is essential to work closely to the work breakdown schedule. One of the keys to a successful project is the way in which the project's aims and plans are communicated to the project team at the implementation stage, so the project manager should gather his or her team at the start of the implementation phase and, using a checklist if necessary, make sure that all are:

SCHEDULE

Calendar weeks			1	2	3	4	5	6	7	8	9	10
Week commencing			20-Apr	27-Apr	04-May	11-May	18-May	25-May	01-Jun	08-Jun	15-Jun	22-Jun
ACTIVITY	Employee days allocated	Who allocated										
Meet stakeholders and gain agreement on activities and timescales												
Review entry criteria for course												
Identify outcome evidence required to evaluate service												
Identify information requirements:												
Course data												
Setting of interviews with course deliverers												
Request and chase key data												
Development of questionaries for:												
Service providers												
Staff												
Setting/aligning of interviews												
One-to-one Interviews												
Review of interviews, identification of commonalities												
Preparation of report												
Interviews with attendees – what worked, etc.												
Interviews with staff, key stakeholders, including commissioners												
Review of key interviews and collation of key issues												
Quantitative analysis of current service provision/outcomes												
Review												
Delivery of final report/presentation												
Weekly review meetings (internal)												
Fortnightly email updates												
Monthly report												
Major reviews												

Figure 2.1

- fully aware of the scope of the project and its desired outcomes
- adequately trained for the tasks planned for them
- not resistant to the project; change often causes resistance and if all the project's team members are not fully on board with the aims of a project then failure will quickly follow – it is vital that a project manager is aware of any resistance or doubts in his or her team and deals with them as soon as possible.

At the kick-off meeting, held after the planning stage has been completed, there should be a comprehensive overview of the project. Obviously, if the team have not formally met at this point they must be introduced and the responsibilities and reporting structure outlined. The project's required outcomes, resources and timing must be made clear. Here the activities that are to commence immediately can be explained in detail and agreement to the tasks and inputs obtained. It is important at this stage to ensure that all team members are fully aware of administrative details, such as how to get in touch with the project leader and other team members, what documentation will be needed and where it is to be kept, and what progress reports are required. Authority limits for resource requests, the reporting structure for problems and risks encountered can also be made clear at this meeting.

After this, work on the tasks in the work breakdown schedule can begin and the project manager must keep the project plans closely to hand so that any deviation from them can be spotted and acted upon and so that progress can be reported on an agreed, regular basis to the project's sponsors.

In addition to communication with the team and with sponsors, it is at this stage that regular communication with the eventual users of the project's objectives comes into play. Here again, it is common to meet resistance. No matter what has been said at the design phase about the essential nature of the projected improvements within the organisation, there is often resistance from the people whose daily working lives will be changed by those improvements. In fact, they will often feel that what is on offer is not an improvement at all. The project manager will not always be able to convince such people of the benefits to them of the project, but it is his or her job to remove any barriers to the project. It may be that a complete buy-in by users is not possible and, in this case, it may be necessary to simply push the changes through with the authority of the project's sponsors as a last resort.

Evaluating the success of your project

The evaluation stage of a project will include, in addition to a comprehensive review of the project, a shutdown phase that will close the project and ensure that no further costs are accrued. The objectives at this stage are:

- To ensure that all the processes set up specifically for the project are completely shut down and that resources that are no longer needed on the project can be allocated elsewhere.
- To establish exactly what was learned during the project. There should be benefits here for the organisation as a whole.
- To review the possibilities for further benefits over and above the project deliverables. As the project has progressed, it may have become apparent that there are other possible projects that need to be evaluated for the future so at this point these should be documented and a decision taken as to how to progress.

A project manager will, at this stage, conduct a full review with team members and also with stakeholders of the project's successes and failures. It should be noted that there is little to be gained from angling this review towards blame. It is preferable that an objective discussion be had that will highlight what worked well – and not so well – and this should define how the organisation proceeds. The manager may wish to do more of some things and less of others.

Of course, the major part of this evaluation stage will be the review of the scale and type of benefits that have been gained and exactly how these compare with the original objectives of the project. There are four main areas that must be considered when measuring the success of a project:

1. Have the objectives been met? This checks the scope of the project, i.e. the amount of work done.
2. Are the sponsors of the project satisfied with the outcome? Specific benefits will have been promised at the outset of the project – for example, this may have been to reduce costs, to increase sales or to remove a problem – and the evaluation of a project will always include a report on how far this goal was met. Benefits achieved must be quantified wherever possible.
3. Was the project delivered on time?
4. Did the project keep to its budget? This should be in terms of all resources used including people hours as well as financial input.

Some common pitfalls

Management performance can always be improved by an awareness of what can go wrong. Before you start a project it will be useful to read through the following list of some of the most common pitfalls so that you can take extra care not to fall:

- Inadequate definition of the project at the start – if you don't really know where you're going, the chances of your getting there are considerably reduced.
- Not making a sufficient business case for the project – this is essential to ensure that everyone is convinced of the need for the project. Half-hearted support from stakeholders can derail a project. A business case will quantify the costs and benefits of a project.
- Lack of communication – if people are left in the dark then results will inevitably be poor.
- Insufficient management time allowed – a project should be distinct from everyday operational roles.
- Inadequate definition of roles and responsibilities – this can only lead to confusion and a poorly run project.
- Lack of control of resources – this can lead to projects costing more than has been budgeted and this is seen as project failure.
- Ignoring constraints – it is vital that the project manager is aware of, and reacts to, constraints.
- Poor definition of the project's outcomes – it is essential to be absolutely clear what the project has to achieve.
- Ignoring risks – all risks must be identified, analysed and managed.

Managing a programme of projects

Managing a programme of projects is essentially a task of co-ordination. It may be that a manager is tasked with being a project manager and also with managing a programme of projects. When managing more than one project at any one time the likelihood of something going seriously wrong is inevitably increased. However, it is possible to manage multiple projects successfully if certain rules are paid extra attention. These include:

1. **Check progress continually** – it is the manager's job to keep track of how each project is going. Even if you only have one major project you will need to do this but with more than one project then this skill is even more important.
2. **Delegation** – it is always important to delegate, but more so if you have various projects going on at the same time.
3. **Prioritise** – make sure that you rank the projects in order of their importance and delivery dates.
4. **Manage expectations** – especially those of stakeholders. Being realistic should never be viewed as admitting defeat.

Let's look at these four aspects of managing multiple projects individually. During the life of a project things will change constantly so regular reviews to ensure that a project is still on track are essential. Progress reports should be built in to the tasks for each member of your team and these could be weekly or monthly depending on the complexity and life of the project and could be written or delivered verbally in a general meeting or a one-to-one meeting. Although you do not want to encourage lengthy reporting that will waste everybody's time, including yours, you need to know, on a regular basis, that the project is keeping on track and that everything that you expected – and planned – to happen is happening. If reports are a routine part of the tasks assigned then your team are more likely to react well to what can be seen as an onerous waste of time. Of course, it is not a waste of time as you, the project manager, must know when things are not going to plan.

A further checkpoint apart from monthly or weekly reviews is the use of milestones built in to the project. A milestone is a distinct point in a project when a report on progress towards the project's deliverables is made. Any project will have minor objectives to achieve on the way to the main objectives and this is when you can check on progress. Has that point been reached on the date that you had planned? Have the results to that point been as expected? Have any problems that could derail the project been uncovered?

When things change you will be able to see what is wrong as part of your regular reviews or milestone checks and it is your job to get the project back on track. It may be necessary to reschedule or re-plan some aspects of your project in response to that change. The ways to get a project back on track include changing your estimates of how long things will take or changing the resources you have allocated. Where your time estimates are found to be slipping, you can examine your plan to see where time can be pulled back. For example, if you have scheduled in a two-day training session or a four-hour meeting, is there any way that you can run these differently so that they take less time? A tightly run meeting for which all the participants are well prepared will always take less time than one where people get the agenda when they arrive and are allowed to chat before getting down to business. Similarly, the time that a training session takes can be reduced by giving out background material before the session and follow-up material for study after the session. If you decide that the way to get a project back on track is by a change in resources, then you will have to choose between changing the people allocated to certain tasks in an attempt to make things happen more quickly or more efficiently, allowing overtime on the project so that more money is allocated, improving the skills of some team members or adding in extra team members. Let's look at these options in turn.

Changing the allocation of tasks can work by ensuring that no one team member is overstretched while another is not working to full capacity. By swapping their tasks around you may find that a better balance is reached and the project will be back on track. However, this will need to be done carefully and with plenty of consultation with the team members involved so that the person who has had a task taken away does not feel that he or she has done something wrong and the person with an increased workload does not feel overwhelmed or resentful.

Allowing overtime on a project where it was not planned from the beginning is a difficult option. This will, of course, get more time on the project from people who are already familiar with what needs to be done, but there are disadvantages. Not only does it increase the cost of the project – and this will need to be made known to the stakeholders – but it can also lead to problems with team members if the amount of overtime needed is excessive.

Improving the skills of one or more team members is often something that will result in a general improvement in a project and bring it back on track. If you find that a team member does not have the skills to perform a task efficiently then it may be possible to quickly bring that person up to speed and ensure that they can keep to their schedules for the remainder of the project. It is also often necessary to add team-building exercises to a project where the team is not functioning well together. A few well-planned activities can make things run much more smoothly and you may be able to pick up time in this way.

The last option – adding members to the team – is often not successful because the team dynamics will change and it can take some time for a new member to get up to speed. Splitting tasks between team members is often problematical as it can actually increase the total amount of time spent on a task because of the communication and extra start-up time required. It will also increase the manager's workload in terms of communications with the increased team.

INSTANT TIP

Although you must keep track of all your projects and know what all the members of your team are doing, resist the temptation to try to do everything yourself or to insist that everything is done exactly as you would do it. You are looking for results, not simply compliance with your instructions.

Delegation is essential. All good managers must admit to themselves that it is impossible to do everything. In fact, one definition of management is 'getting things done through other people'. So, management inevitably includes other people doing things alongside you. It is the manager's job to decide who does what and when. There is no need to feel guilty about passing work on to others – the more you delegate to members of your team, the more they will learn and develop – in addition to you getting your own job done more effectively. Two things that will ensure that delegation works for you are to delegate whatever will save you time and to delegate to the right person. Deciding what will save you time is probably an easy task but deciding who to delegate those tasks to is more difficult. Hopefully you will have trained your team and will know who is capable of what so, as long as you don't delegate at the last minute (which can lead to panic and lack of preparation), you should be able to delegate effectively. Don't forget that you can delegate a task upwards too, so consider your boss or people in other departments when you have a task that might be outside your team's skills. Matching the task to be delegated to the skills available is key to good delegation.

Learning how to prioritise your work will ensure that you do not merely keep busy. You will do what is most important and/or what is most urgent first rather than just picking a task and doing it. You should review each individual task before you even make a start on it, asking yourself whether it is important or urgent, or both or neither, and then deal with the task accordingly. Using the urgent/important rule you will deal with tasks as follows:

- If you decide something is urgent and important you need to do it immediately.
- If it is urgent but not important you can choose to delegate it or plan to do it yourself later.
- If a task is important but not urgent you can put it in your diary for later.
- If you decide a task is neither important nor urgent then you don't need to do it.

Managing expectations is often one of the more difficult aspects of a manager's role. It is natural, sometimes, to want to present an optimistic face to the world and to assure everyone that things are going to plan. But this can be a mistake. If you have uncovered a flaw in a plan and realise that it will affect the deliverables of the project then you need to analyse the situation and make stakeholders aware that things have changed – and why. In large, formal projects there will usually be a number of phase reviews planned. At this point the project manager will review the progress of the project and produce a report for the project sponsor and other stakeholders. This is a critical point as the sponsor may decide to cancel or reduce the project if things are not going to plan or, if the deliverables are there as planned, may decide to increase the project or simply give the go-ahead for the next phase. In smaller, less formal projects, this phase review may not be a regular item but where things are not going to plan it is better to warn all concerned that, for example, the project may not be completed on time or the planned objectives will not be fully met.

Of course, doing all these things will not guarantee success if you are not able to manage your own time effectively, so time management becomes of prime importance if you are managing a variety of projects at any one time. You will also need to manage the time of your team members to a certain extent. Every worker needs to be able to manage his or her own time but it is part of the manager's role to keep team members on track and to offer help and guidance as to how best to use the time available to each worker. Let's look at a few basics of personal time management that you should keep in mind – and practise – in order to keep on track.

Self-management techniques

Use a diary

Record deadlines, start dates for tasks, meetings and so on for both yourself and your team members. Not only will efficient use of a diary ensure that you are aware of important deadlines but, in conjunction with 'to do' lists (described below), it will also help to make you aware of how you spend your time. The Outlook Calendar or similar tool can be very good for setting reminders, planning meetings etc. Knowing where your time is going is essential if you are to make more efficient use of it.

Make a 'to do' list

Update it every day. Put on it everything that you must do that day and also anything you are considering doing. Then go through the list and decide on urgency and importance as described above. This will allow you to reduce your 'to do' list by delegating some items and deciding not to do other things at all and it will focus your attention on what must be done first, i.e. anything that is both urgent and important.

Keep details to hand

Make sure that you keep contact details, phone numbers and so on to hand. You might choose to use a laptop contact management programme for this. This can be useful as you will have email details in the same place or you can simply store telephone numbers in your mobile phone. However, some people only feel comfortable with contact details in written format and use a small book that they carry with them at all times. Whatever works for you, use it.

Get organised

If your desk and office are so untidy that you cannot lay your hands on an important piece of paper quickly then you will not work efficiently. It is worth spending a little time to restore some order. Do not, however, allow 'getting organised' to become what you do on a regular basis. This is known as a displacement activity and could easily take the place of doing any 'real work'. Often, an overload of paperwork is at the root of the problem. One way of tackling this is to deal with current incoming paperwork immediately rather than stacking it in ever-higher piles. So, when paper lands on your desk decide immediately what needs to be done with it and then do it. The four options for every piece of paper are: take action on it; file it; pass it on to someone else; throw it away. In dealing with the ones that you decide are for action by you, include these on your 'to do' list according to their urgency and importance. When you've got the incoming paperwork under control then you can start to tackle the backlog by picking up each piece of paper on your desk just once and making a decision on it there and then. If you were to keep track of how many times you've handled those pieces of paper forming tottering piles on your desk – and maybe on the floor and any other horizontal surface – you would probably find that you've looked at most of them many times but done nothing. This is just time wasting and getting out of that habit is the best way to control paperwork.

Control your use of the phone

For outgoing calls, group them together and have a period or two of time set aside in your day to make all your calls (make them times when people are likely to be available), prepare yourself with all the information you will need and get them over with in one – or two – spells. Only make calls that are really necessary – could you send an email instead for instance, as that will cut out the unnecessary chat? Try to use emails when you know that someone will take up your time if you call. You should also try to cut down the number of phone calls you receive. Although some calls are essential and will actually help you to do your job, incoming calls can be intrusive and stop you doing your job effectively so it can be a good idea to let people know that you can only take incoming calls at certain times during the day and that the remainder of the working day your answering machine/voicemail will be on.

Learn to say no!

It is not always possible to take on more and more projects, so if you feel that taking on another one would jeopardise an existing project, say so. You should decide whether what you are being asked to do fits in with your priorities. So, if it is something that would advance one of your projects or would make your life easier or improve it in some way, then you should probably say yes to the request. If, however, what you are being asked to do is someone else's priority and does not help you, then say no without feeling any guilt.

SUMMARY

Remember that this book is not a project management book – look in the recommended further reading section at the end of this book for resources that explore this very complicated subject in a much greater level of detail.

We started by clarifying the difference between processes and projects and how they interact, and found that a process is a set of actions whereas a project is used to solve a problem by changing a sequence of actions or setting up a new sequence of actions.

Managing Business Process Improvement (BPI) requires an analysis of the processes and how they interact to achieve the objectives of the organisation. Essentially, BPI answers the question, 'How can we do it better?'

When starting a project two things were seen to be of prime importance:

- choosing the right team – with a variety of skills according to the requirements of the project
- setting clear objectives and making them known to all involved from the start

We then looked at the different stages of a project:

- the initiation stage, when the scope of a project will be decided and a lot of preparatory research is carried out
- the planning stage, which shows how you will achieve your objectives

(Continued)

(Continued)

- the preparation of a work breakdown structure
- the implementation stage, when systems are put in place
- the evaluation and shutdown stage.

We then looked at some of the common pitfalls of managing a project, including a lack of definition and control, and poor communication.

Finally we examined the problems of having to manage more than one project. Here we looked at the importance of time management and of delegation and the need to manage everyone's expectations while keeping track of each individual project and setting priorities.

ACTION CHECKLIST

In order to further your understanding of how a project is managed, it can be useful to look more closely at an actual example with which you are familiar:

1. Identify a small project that you have undertaken in the course of your job.
2. Break this project down in to the different stages (initiation, planning, preparation of a work breakdown structure, implementation, evaluation and shutdown).
3. Look at what each member of your project team contributed. Analyse the skills that each brought to the project.
4. Now evaluate the success – or otherwise – of your project. Did it achieve its objectives? Were your sponsors satisfied with the outcome?
5. What would you have done differently if you had to carry out the project again?

03

Who are your customers?

There is no doubt that the commercial world is becoming ever more competitive and if an organisation does not know its customers and fully understand them, their requirements and their motivations they will find it impossible to achieve any degree of success. It may be useful here to define just what a customer is. Is it just someone – maybe you – who walks into a shop and hands over money in exchange for a new dress or some chocolate? Or could it be something more complicated than that? At its most basic, it is an individual or organisation who exchanges one benefit for another. This definition certainly covers the shopper we mentioned, but it also includes one department in an organisation supplying another department with a service or product and it also includes organisations purchasing goods or services in exchange for payment. To establish a customer–supplier relationship, each side must be gaining something from the transaction. So, who are your organisation's customers?

Finding out about your customers

To be successful, every organisation must know who their customers – and potential customers – are and what they want and need from their suppliers. If you do not understand what your customers want and need then you will not be able to satisfy those wants and needs. You will need to understand exactly what your customers gain from using your products or services. This must involve a comprehensive view of your customers' motivations and all the things that will impact on their buying decisions. It will not be very useful to simply look at what they buy and see the benefit to them of the product or service you have supplied. You will need to understand fully why they buy what they buy. There will be all sorts of reasons for their purchasing decision such as:

- price
- availability
- advertising you have done and that customers have been exposed to
- cultural influences
- the current economic situation
- what your competitors are offering
- your salesperson's performance
- quality of your product
- your service levels
- your organisation's relationships with your customers
- emotional reasons such as fear or greed.

Having considered the possible reasons why your customers buy from you, you will need to look at the data that your organisation has about your customers. In particular you can find out who they are – what size of company, where they are and what their business is – and also what they buy from you – the particular products, how many they buy and how often. You are aiming at reaching a better understanding of what your customers buy and why. Of course, written data that your organisation has compiled will not tell you the whole story. You should communicate too – with your customers and with the people within your organisation who deal with them. Find out answers to the following:

- Why do they buy what they buy?
- Why do they not buy more?
- What do they buy from other companies?
- What is important to them?
- What do they plan to buy in the future?

INSTANT TIP

Do your customers buy similar products from other suppliers? Don't know? Then ask them. You may be able to sell more of your own products if you know more about your customers' buying behaviour.

When you are in possession of comprehensive information about your customers you will then be in a position to predict their behaviour – although this will not always be totally successful – and to tailor your products, services and approach accordingly. There will be more about finding out why your customers buy from you later in this chapter.

Are you a customer?

Of course, we are all customers of many organisations. We all buy food, clothing, utilities, transport in some shape or form, and perhaps holidays, furniture and property. But have you considered that you are also a customer of other departments of the organisation for which you work? Going back to the simple definition above, a customer is an individual or organisation which exchanges one benefit for another so, of course you are a customer in that sense as you will no doubt be relying, for example, on the invoicing department to send out invoices for the goods you have sold or the production department to come up with the goods that your customers want. These goods and services are the internal customer system and it is useful to consider how good or bad this customer experience is. Do you get a fair deal? Examining these customer experiences both within and outside your own organisations is a valuable tool to use when trying to improve customer service or sales totals within your own department.

INSTANT TIP

Whenever you make a purchase from an outside organisation or receive a service or product from another department, try to analyse why you made the purchase and assess whether or not it was a fair exchange. This should help you in understanding your customers.

Why do your customers buy from you?

Now that you know a little about your customers the picture should be becoming clearer as to why they buy from you. This will help you either to do more of the same if the conclusions you draw are positive or point you in the right direction as to necessary changes if you find that there are areas that need improvement. This will form your framework for a marketing strategy and will also give you vital information about sales trends, requirements for the future, stock levels necessary and resources needed in terms of both personnel and product. This will, of course, enable financial forecasts to be made for the organisation.

A useful starting point is to consider the three different types of customers separately. The three types are:

1. consumers – individual customers buying in a domestic situation
2. business to business
3. internal.

So, how do you find out what makes your customers buy from you? Why from your organisation rather than from your competitors? Why have they bought the particular product or service? What were their motivations?

If you are not already in possession of extensive reports about the sales your organisation has made, you will need to gather the data that your organisation will – or certainly should – have regarding the amounts of all the items in your range that have been sold and what each customer bought and when. Of course, this data will vary according to your organisation's normal business practices. It will also be affected by whether the sales have taken place in a consumer (private individual) situation, a business-to-business environment or whether the exchanges are taking place in an internal market.

There are many factors that make your customers buy from you – or not buy from you – and it is only by fully understanding these factors that you can increase your sales or implement a Customer Relationship Management strategy.

If you are selling your products or services to individuals then you will need to be aware of the following general, external factors that can affect your customers' buying decisions:

Economic situation

This will affect your customers' buying power as well as their attitudes towards your product. For example, in times of a recession many people may decrease their spending on luxury goods – even if their income has not significantly changed.

Media

The information that is available to your customers via television, magazines and newspapers and so on can increase or decrease their desire for your product or service. Advertising is part of the marketing mix and can be very important to your company. More about this later in this chapter.

Technology

Constant changes in technology will give your customers more choice and may decrease their need for your product or may affect the amount of money they have available to spend on your product if they are spending more on new technology.

Who makes the buying decision?

More than one person may be involved in the buying decision. In years gone by, for example, men were the main decision makers when buying cars for the family. Now women have much more of a say in such decisions. Also, children are given greater prominence now in buying decisions for items such as holidays, cars, food and clothing.

Competition

What your competitors are doing will inevitably impact on your sales. You will need to be fully aware of what types of organisations you are competing with and what products and services they are offering as well as the prices and availability.

Age

Many products are aimed at a specific age group. This includes holidays, types of clothing, books and even some cars or foods, in addition to specific products such as prams or stair lifts.

Gender

Some products are made for use by either solely men or solely women, but it should be remembered that products are often actually purchased by both sexes, for example men's clothing is commonly bought by women for men.

Income

This has an obvious effect on your customers' purchasing power and may well affect your product offer.

Where they live

Someone living in a large city will have different needs – for example, for transport – than someone living in an isolated rural village.

Marital status

Whether your customers are single, married, partnered, divorced or widowed will have an affect on their purchases. For example, a single person may well buy a different car from a married couple or food products in different sized packs.

Children

Apart from customers with a family buying the obvious children's products such as clothing and toys, their buying decisions will also be influenced by the children and by their perceived needs.

Occupation

This factor is closely related to the next one – socio-economic group. However, certain occupations raise needs for specific products, e.g. barristers buy wigs and plumbers buy tools and plumbing materials. If your product or service is occupation-specific then this factor will be an important one in your customer research.

Socio-economic standing

Although these groupings have lost some of their relevance since their development as a way of analysing social class in the early 1950s, they are still widely used in marketing research. These groups are:

A	Professional people
B	Middle management
C1	Junior management
C2	Skilled manual
D	Semi-skilled and unskilled manual workers
E	Casual workers and those dependent on the state (unemployed, long-term sick etc.)

Location

If your product or service is location-specific then you should be aware of this. For example, if your customer base is largely confined to the local area around the organisation then there is little point in advertising further afield – unless, of course, you feel that you can expand your customer base into other areas.

Credit

The increasing availability of consumer credit in recent years may have affected your customers' ability to purchase your product.

Home ownership

People who own their own homes may have different needs from someone who rents their home. Also, the type of property they own may be an indicator of other factors that affect buying decisions such as income, types of product needed for bigger or smaller homes and so on.

Interests

Depending on the type of product or service that you supply, this may enable you to tailor your product to suit the customer or to add to your product range according to what it is likely they will buy.

INSTANT TIP

Now, without any preparation, write down a description of your organisation's typical customer. Save your notes until you've finished your analysis of your customer base. This will show how familiar you are with your customers and how much you need to learn.

If the sales you are analysing are straightforward sales of a product or service by your organisation to another organisation your customers will have other motivations for their buying decisions:

- Does your product produce a benefit for your customer? Usually, the main reason for making the decision to purchase in the case of a business is to improve the bottom line. You need to understand how profitable your product is for your customer and what their organisation is trying to achieve.
- You need to be aware of who the buyer is. You may know the name of the person who holds the position of 'Buyer', but do you know who else may influence the decision to buy? This is important to know because it will obviously affect your approach to your customer and give you different sets of needs that you will have to fulfil.

If the 'sales' are to internal customers there will be less competition but a variety of different motivations to consider. These will include:

- **Reputation** – if your department has gained a good reputation in the past, maybe by providing a quicker, more responsive service than other departments, then it will have an advantage over others when needed and may get better service in return when there are problems to solve.

- **Better staff** – a department that can offer a high level of service, has good management and a reputation for quality will find it easier to recruit good quality staff and to keep existing staff. This will ensure high morale and a continued high performance.
- **Cooperation** – dealing successfully with one department can make relations with other departments easier.
- **Attitudes** – this works two ways. Good internal customer relationships will result in better attitudes being shown on a daily basis towards the department's staff and also by the department's staff themselves.
- **Bonuses** – in addition to all the benefits as detailed above a department may be motivated by the possibility of bonuses, increased pay, improved working conditions or other rewards that may come to a successful department.

One last thing to consider when looking at why your customers buy from you is branding. How important is your brand and how much effort is put into creating and maintaining it? Brand can be defined as the image that a product has and can increase the value of a product. Brand management is a way of gaining a niche position in your market. Clever marketing, including how the advertising portrays and positions the product or service that your organisation is offering, can create a brand thereby changing a product into something that is desired. As a result, the product will command a considerably higher price than it would have without the brand management.

INSTANT TIP

Now that you have plenty of information about exactly who your customers are, write a description of your organisation's typical customer and compare it with the one that you wrote earlier. Were you right? If not, spend some time considering where you went wrong – and why.

Having gathered the necessary data you can then go about the interesting task of analysing why your customers have behaved as they have.

Analysing customer behaviour

When you have analysed why your customers have bought what they have, you will need to use the information to help you to decide how to deal with your customers to maximise sales. The aim is to make sure that your marketing efforts are directed to the right place. Not every individual or every organisation will want or need your products and, of course, approaching everyone would be impossible. If you try to contact too many people then you will not be concentrating on the people who are most likely to buy. By directing your efforts to fewer people – but ones who are likely to need your product because they are similar to your existing customers – then you will be in a position to significantly increase your sales.

Depending on the information that you have and the conclusions you can draw from the information you have found, you may also decide to change your product or service or to try to increase your customer base by doing more of the same but in a different area or by diversifying.

Your challenge in this task will be to understand fully the opportunities offered by the data you have and then to make the changes that will allow you to take up these opportunities. Understanding the impact that your actions can have on your sales results is essential at this point and you will need to assess the impact of your customers' response to your future activity.

Developing a customer strategy

Having analysed just who your customers are and why they buy from you, you will be in a position to develop a strategy for ensuring that the customer care in your organisation is as good as it can be and is organised in a way that makes it work at all times, in all circumstances.

Developing a strategy involves deciding on the approach that will be taken to achieve the standards you have set and to meet your objectives. It will include timescales and should set out the benefits for the organisation. There are a number of steps to take in establishing an effective customer care strategy:

- Look at how the rest of the market does it.
- Decide where you are at now.
- Decide where you want to be – and when.
- Set standards.
- Decide on a customer care plan.
- List the tasks necessary to implement and maintain the customer care plan.
- Allocate these tasks.
- Implement the plan.
- Monitor results.
- Change the plan where necessary.
- Monitor at regular intervals.

Let's look at these stages in a bit more detail. If you're getting ideas together as to how to improve customer care in your organisation, then an ideal place to start is by looking at how your competitors do it. It should be obvious to you, if you know your market and your competitors, just who is doing a good job and would be worth emulating. Consider how these possible examples deal with customer care. How is their customer care perceived in the market? Have they got a reputation for offering value for money? How well do they fulfil orders? Are their customers kept informed? What is their after-sales service like? If your own customer care is in need of improvement, then a close examination of what is going on in the market in which you compete will undoubtedly show you where you need to concentrate your efforts.

Decide where you are at now. You can do this by getting together data on how much repeat business you get, how many complaints you receive (it is useful to split this into product complaints and complaints about how customers have been dealt with by your employees), how long your order-to-delivery cycle is, the amount of goods returned, and how many times you currently contact your customers. Keep all these details as they will be useful in the future when you are reviewing improvements.

Decide where you want to be – and when. At this point you will set your objectives. You must decide what you are aiming at in terms of the standards of customer care to be met and when you aim to meet them. Of course, all the objectives must be SMART – Specific, Measurable, Achievable, Realistic and Time-based – so write them down and make sure that they pass the 'SMART test'. The other test your objectives must pass is that they have to give you a competitive advantage. Meeting standards almost always increases your costs so setting standards without making sure that you get some benefit from meeting them is pointless and costly.

If you set standards for your customer care based on what you are currently achieving and a set of standards that represent what you want to achieve you will know when the improvements you are looking for come about. You will need to be familiar with the best practices in use in your industry or market and set standards for the future based on these. Setting standards like this often convinces people within the organisation who may have been satisfied with the status quo that improvement really is necessary and possible. Each aspect of customer care can be given targets. You can even measure non-financial factors – for example, a time agreed for your order-to-delivery cycle or the frequency of visits to customers. For more information on setting standards related to customer service see the section on Key Performance Indicators in Chapter 5.

Decide on a customer care plan. This is where you need to get down to detail and pull the plan together. Think about all the different elements of the changes you are going to make and keep your objectives and your customers very firmly in mind. At this stage you will also have to decide on the resources – staff and budget – that you will want, or be able to, commit to the proposed plan. Your plan should cover the following:

- What you want to achieve – lay out the improvements point by point and also why you feel that the extra work is justified.
- How you will achieve it – detail the methods you will use. For example, if your plan involves extra contact with customers, specify exactly how this contact will be made, when and by whom.
- Who will help you to achieve it – you should be specific about the staff that will be responsible for each stage and element of your plan.
- When you want to achieve it – this involves specifying a start date for your plan and also a deadline for when the objectives will have been achieved. Remember, this deadline will be when you will need to produce results and a report that quantifies your success.
- Resources you will need – include the cost of any new equipment, stationery and marketing materials you may

need and also the number of employee hours that will be devoted to producing the benefits.

● Quantify the benefits – the 'bottom line' is all that many very senior managers will know about the new customer care strategy and this is how it will be 'sold' to all those in the organisation who are not directly involved in making it work.

Next you need to list the tasks necessary to implement and maintain the customer care plan. This stage increases the level of detail that is necessary and it will be helpful to carry out this task alongside the people who will be carrying out the work. Don't forget that training may be necessary to bring your team's skills up to the level required to ensure your plans can be carried out and this training should be included in the plan and time allowed as appropriate.

Allocate these tasks to individual team members and also specify who will be responsible for overseeing each stage of the plan.

Now it is time to implement the plan. This is obviously a very important part of the process of improving customer care. Nothing will happen despite all the research and the time and effort that have gone into setting objectives and developing the plan unless it is put into action. Someone has to do something after all the planning. As the instigator of the plan you will need to be present during this stage – and will, no doubt, have your own allocated tasks to carry out. You will need to be available to answer questions, to smooth over areas where things do not go entirely to plan, to revise your plans if necessary and to encourage your team. However, do not make them too aware of your presence as very close supervision when carrying out new tasks can be daunting and counter-productive. This is, of course, part of the delicate balancing act that is management.

Monitoring results is an essential part of a new customer care strategy. As always, if you do not monitor and measure the results, especially in the early stages of a new plan, it will be impossible to know if you are on the right track. You will need to decide exactly how you are going to measure the results when you are setting the standards. You must have specific targets set that are quantifiable so that you can be certain whether or not the standards have been met. It will then be a relatively simple task to compare data from before and after implementation.

When you monitor results at the end of the implementation phase, it should take the form of a major review to make sure that everything is going to plan and that the benefits you anticipated are being realised. Here you will need to recognise achievement and hard work by the people involved and publicise the gains, benefits and improvements that have been made by the organisation. You will also need to ensure that the changes, if successful, are embedded as new work practices and that systems are in place to check that results continue to be produced. An important part of your monitoring systems will be to get customer feedback on a regular basis. It can be useful at the planning stages to develop questionnaires to send out to customers at different times to check on progress. As always, you will need to take care that this does not become an annoying intrusion into your customers' working day.

Of course, if you find that your objectives are not being met, you will need to have contingency plans in place to put things right. These are usually the result of a brainstorming session with your team where you look at everything that could go wrong and develop a solution to the problem to be used if it should occur.

Do not be afraid to change the plan where necessary. In business, plans can never be cast in stone so you must be willing to change what isn't working. If you are not prepared to make changes to your plan there is little point in setting standards. You've set your standards and if you're not meeting them within the time allowed you will need to find out why and then put the required changes in place.

Ensuring that standards are being met is not a one-off job. You must put in place a regular programme of checks that will keep you on track. This can also be a helpful way to monitor trends so that you can see continual improvement. You can develop areas where you are getting good results – that is, do more of the same – and change things where it is not working so well or where progress slows down over time. Above all, do not be tempted to simply measure your results over time and then ignore the data that is produced. Measuring is only useful if someone takes action in response to the results.

Finally, remember that why customers buy from you now may not be the reason behind buying decisions in the future. Spotting market trends is an ideal way to get one step ahead of your competitors. If, from your analysis of your customers' current behaviour and from talking with your customers, you can start to predict what they will need in the future, you will have hit a winning formula. These changes can be relatively small but spotting them early on in the cycle will almost always prove profitable. There may be a small change such as how they will want to order in the future or the colours or sizes that will change. Whatever it is, you need to get into a way of thinking about what your customers want so that you can be the first in the market with something that satisfies new requirements.

SUMMARY

In this chapter we concentrated on the importance of knowing who your customers are and what you need to find out about customers and their wants and needs.

We found that customers can be put into three categories – internal, individual/consumer and business to business – and that each will have different priorities leading to different wants and needs. Internal customers will be influenced by their reputation within the organisation, by the need to recruit and retain good quality staff and possibly by bonuses that may become payable. There are lots of factors that need to be taken into account when selling to individual consumers

(Continued)

(Continued)

including their age, gender, location and socio-economic standing. For business-to-business customers you should take into account that there will often be more than one person making the buying decision and that they will be looking for benefits for their organisation from your product.

We then looked at the different stages of developing a strategy for customer care – deciding where you are now and where you want to be, setting standards, implementing and maintaining a customer care plan and allocating the tasks that will make the improvement happen. The results must then be monitored on an ongoing basis and changes made wherever and whenever necessary.

ACTION CHECKLIST

In this important chapter we asked the question, 'Who are your customers?'. The following exercises will help you to find out who exactly your customers are:

1. Find out exactly what data your organisation keeps regarding its customers. This may require you to contact various departments.
2. Find out who your top ten customers are in terms of value of products or services purchased.
3. Do you know who makes the buying decision in the case of each of these major customers?
4. Give three reasons why your major customers buy from your organisation.
5. What do you know about your customers' perceptions of your customer service?

04

How can you make your organisation focus on its customers?

The service a customer gets from any organisation will have a huge effect on his or her buying decisions. For this reason it is obviously essential for all organisations to make efforts to focus on customers and to be aiming for continual improvements in this area.

In recent years the emphasis in marketing has shifted from concentrating on simply making a sale to using excellence in customer service to gain – and keep – customers. This has led to a more customer-focused approach and 'relationship marketing' has come to the fore. This book will show you some of the ways in which customer service and developing relationships with customers can be managed. In this chapter we will look at what makes customer care so important and how an organisation can become more customer focused.

Fostering customer-based values in your organisation

Putting the customer first is something that can be achieved in any organisation. This attitude must start from the top and be well publicised throughout the organisation so that no one is in any doubt about where senior management's priorities lie. The reasons behind this emphasis must be made clear, i.e. that good customer service wins business and leads to profitability.

One of the most important contributors to good customer service – and one that can ruin a company's reputation in seconds – is the attitude that staff have to customers. If there are any problems in this area, management must drive a programme aimed at achieving high levels of customer care. This includes:

Making it known that customer service has a high priority

This can be done in a number of ways and, indeed, will involve various measures to ensure that the message gets across to all members of staff. A mission statement is one way of doing this. It is usually signed by the Managing Director or most senior person in the organisation and should put customer satisfaction very firmly in the spotlight. Most senior management recognise that customer service should have priority because of its enormous impact on profitability but this can get lost in the day-to-day job of producing goods or providing services. Management must act to show that it should always be at the forefront.

Planning for good customer service

Evidence of a comprehensive plan to improve customer service levels can bring about change in attitudes, while also providing the systems to make high standards possible. The systems put in place must obviously be customer friendly in order to achieve the main aim of the changes but if they are also staff friendly in that they are easy to operate, then this will further the aim of fostering the right attitudes in staff. Although systems are important, the personal touch must be retained and encouraged in any dealings with customers. One of the most frustrating excuses that a customer can receive for something not being done correctly is that 'the computer's down'. Make sure back-up procedures are in place, and familiar to all staff, to be used when there are technical problems so that your customers never have to be subjected to this.

Employing the right staff

When recruiting customer service staff in particular it is essential that people with the right attitudes to customer service are engaged, although the right attitude to customers will be useful in everyone in the organisation.

Staff training

There are plenty of training courses available that teach customer-handling skills and it is well worthwhile to offer this to anyone who struggles to any degree with this aspect of their job.

Installing the right systems

This aspect of customer service falls into two areas. First there are the systems that your staff use on a day-to-day basis to do their jobs and second there are the systems that you can put in place for customers that will improve your product offer. This latter category can include customer help lines – preferably free – and customer loyalty schemes that reward repeat orders. The systems used by staff should all be geared towards making it easy to satisfy customers and, of course, all members of staff who have to use them should be thoroughly familiar with them.

Dealing with customer complaints

The right attitude to customer complaints can greatly improve customer service. If staff can be encouraged to welcome complaints as a chance to get a customer's feedback this will be a step in the right direction. They can then improve the customer's view of the organisation by how they put things right for them. It should be remembered that if a customer doesn't complain to their supplier they will more than likely mention their problem to friends or colleagues – giving your organisation a poor reputation but not giving the organisation the chance to solve the problem. The main way of getting feedback from customers who have a complaint about your product or service is a call to the customer after delivery has taken place to check that they are satisfied with the product. There are also other ways to make it easy for customers to contact the organisation after they have made a purchase, such as freepost cards included with the delivery, free customer help lines, money back guarantees and customer service desks that are widely publicised so that customers know how to contact the company.

Putting problems right

Staff handling customer complaints will quickly become demoralised if they continually have to deal with calls about the same type of problem. When a complaint has been dealt with for the customer it should then be dealt with for the organisation. The issue should be investigated and a solution put in place.

INSTANT TIP

Always reward staff when they beat customer expectations. The reward does not have to be huge but the recognition does. So publicise within your organisation all examples of exceptional customer service – maybe have a 'customer service employee of the month' award or give vouchers or a small bonus on a regular basis.

Communicating with customers

A major part of your customer care programme must be devoted to how you communicate with your customers. You must ensure that all staff that have any customer contact – face-to-face, by letter, email or by telephone – are well trained in how to communicate effectively. They also need to understand fully what the organisation offers to its customers and to have all the information necessary to give customers what they want, including answering queries and complaints efficiently and effectively. You should have a two-pronged approach to this need for suitable staff

– recruiting staff who are customer-focused and then making sure that their training is tailored towards satisfying your customers.

Customer care can be improved by increasing the amount of communication members of your organisation have with customers. Here are some ways to make contact with your customers:

- **Get face-to-face with your customers** – this doesn't just mean that your salespeople need to make more appointments (too many of these can be annoying to customers) but can include going to conferences, networking meetings and exhibitions where you know your customers are likely to be. This can bring you closer to your customers. Not only will you develop relationships and understand more about what they want but also you will have the opportunity to spread the word about new products, developments within your organisation, efforts to improve customer service and so on. You may also think it appropriate to implement a programme of management visits to larger customers. Getting people from different disciplines together can be beneficial to both organisations. So, for example, a visit by your production manager to talk to your customer's buyer or finance people may bring out some very useful information about exactly what your customer wants.

- **Conduct a survey** – this can be a seemingly casual question asked when their order is being taken or a full-blown formal survey aimed at finding out what they really think about your products and services.

- **Start a newsletter** – these are becoming increasingly popular with the prevalence of email as this makes it a very cost-effective way of getting in touch with a large number of people. The most important point to remember when producing a newsletter for your organisation is to make it useful. Don't be tempted to make it just another form of advertising. If all you put in the newsletter is internal company news or you make it a blurb about how wonderful your organisation is, then most customers will immediately delete your newsletter as soon as it hits their inbox or throw it in the bin if you post it to them. Then your time, money and effort will have been wasted. To make a newsletter useful you should include case studies that show how other organisations have overcome problems that your customers may also have, tips and ideas that will help them to run their businesses, articles of interest to people in your market sector as well as new product launch information. It should go without saying that your newsletter should be published regularly – preferably monthly – and it should arrive on schedule, proving your organisation's reliability.

- **Make special offers** – offers limited to existing customers will make them feel special by showing them you think of them as special and will increase their feelings of loyalty towards your organisation.
- **Follow up complaints** – done well, this can cement relationships with customers. If you have resolved a complaint successfully, then a quick phone call to check that all is well can produce a positive reaction from your customer.

Case study

Fast-food restaurants chain McDonald's has a philosophy that if you deal with a customer's complaint successfully, you will win repeat business. They could even be said to like complaints as it gives them a chance to put things right and, by getting it right, win some repeat business.

This demonstrates the importance of training employees to listen and look for problems and then deal with them promptly and effectively. This should be written into the customer care plan so that it happens every time a complaint is made. Good customer service is essential to get repeat business. It is a cost-effective way of ensuring repeat business from existing customers.

Remember to always keep customers informed of product developments. It is imperative that you are continually reviewing your product offer and that you announce any upgrades and additional services to your existing customers. Also, find out what your customers want from you. Ask them the question, 'What else would you like to buy from us that you can't right now?' If you can satisfy their requests, you will keep that customer.

The importance of repeat business

To ensure year on year growth of a business an organisation must always pay attention to their existing customers. Although no organisation can afford to ignore the acquisition of new customers, it is essential that you put effort into retaining, and increasing the sales from, existing customers. The main reason for this is that acquiring new customers is very costly – far more expensive in terms of effort and resources – than retaining existing ones. The way to ensure repeat business is to:

- keep customers satisfied
- ask them what they want from you that they currently don't get
- develop additional products or services
- communicate with your customers.

All these things are provided by good customer service and will ensure that you get a steady stream of orders from your existing customers. Only when you've got the service offering right for your existing customers should you try to win new ones. With poor service you will lose customers.

The second point in considering the importance of repeat business is that if you have a well-established customer base that repeatedly comes back to you for more of the products they have previously ordered then that customer base is the perfect place to start in trying to increase sales. There are three ways to do this:

1. **Cross selling** – this requires a knowledge of why your customers buy the products that they buy from you and what other products they may also need. With this information you may be able to recommend and sell to them other products that they will also find useful.
2. **Up-selling** – this is where you have other, more profitable products in your range that would be better for the customer. Again, you need to understand your customers' requirements to be able to do this.
3. **Selling more of the same** – if you know that a customer regularly places an order at a particular time of the month, for example, you could give them a call or email a couple of weeks earlier to encourage them to order more frequently. This could ensure that they never run out of your product and therefore maximise your sales.

Customer expectations and requirements

At the heart of any good customer care programme is a thorough understanding of customers' expectations and requirements. This understanding informs not only how you set up a customer service department but also the marketing strategy for the whole business. Knowing what the customers want in terms of not just product but service before and after the sale will enable you to maximise sales and profit. It will also enable your organisation to retain customers. It is imperative that you do the research into what your customers want and how they perceive your product rather than just assume that because they are buying from you they are fully satisfied. Let's see how this worked for a small manufacturing company.

Case study

The company manufactured a highly technical product and generally offered a good level of customer service. However, when they lost a major customer they realised that they had not fully understood their customer's requirements and had assumed that the orders would continue to be placed at agreed rates. They felt that the quality and technical specification of their product was superior to their competitors. When they investigated why they had lost a customer who was so important to them they discovered that the customer was now purchasing a similar product but that the technical specification – and the price being charged – was considerably lower than theirs. Their investigations within the company also identified failings in sales staff and departments who were not communicating fully with each other. They set about improving staff training and setting up internal systems to ensure better inter-departmental communication. They were not able to reduce their prices by much but, after a few months, they approached the former customer with a revised offering, emphasising the technical back-up that was included in the slightly lower price and also informing the customer that they had revised and improved their customer service procedures. The newly trained sales staff that put together and delivered this presentation had prepared well and enjoyed the challenge of trying to win back the customer.

Their efforts paid off after a number of visits when the customer gradually started to order products from them again. The MD said 'Departments communicate better using the new systems we implemented, the sales staff's performance improved so much with the correct training that we were also able to gain new customers, increasing our market share by just over 10 per cent in the year since we started the exercise and we are now very conscious that we need to keep up the effort to understand our customers' needs. We will be repeating the exercise on a regular basis from now on.'

SUMMARY

In this chapter we examined how an organisation can make sure that it focuses on its customers. The main thrust of this is that senior management must make it clear that customer service is their main priority and that the right staff must be recruited and trained to deal with customers.

There are almost limitless ways of keeping in touch with your customers. Here we examined more face to-face contact – perhaps by attending exhibitions and networking meetings – plus a programme of management visits, introducing a company newsletter, making special offers and following up all complaints and customer orders.

(Continued)

(Continued)

An examination of the importance of repeat business followed and how customer service can be instrumental in ensuring a high level of repeat business that can maintain sales and increase profitability.

We finished the chapter with a look at what our customers expect from us and how knowing this can retain existing customers and win new ones.

ACTION CHECKLIST

1. Assess how customer service is viewed in your organisation. Is it the number one priority?
2. If customer service is not given a high priority in your organisation, what do you think could be done to improve the situation?
3. How many ways does your organisation communicate with its customers? Can you think of other ways it could do so?
4. What training is offered in your organisation that specifically concentrates on customer service and attitudes towards customers?
5. Think about your main customer's expectations and requirements.

05

Do you have customer service problems?

Although it is sometimes obvious that an organisation has customer service problems, it is possible that poor results are attributed to something else – bad salesmanship, a downturn in the market etc. When an organisation wants to improve sales one of the first things that should be tackled is customer service. If the initial contact with your organisation by customers is poor you will not get their business. This means that not only did you lose out on that one order but also you lost the chance to win repeat business in the future as it is highly unlikely that they will try again. And you may not even know that that potential customer tried and failed to deal with your company. If your customer service in general is poor then your sales will not be as high as perhaps your products and prices would normally allow.

So, how will you know if you have customer service problems? One way, of course, is the number of complaints you receive from customers but sometimes falling sales can be entirely as a result of poor customer service and often this is not spotted until it is too late to put it right.

It will be useful here to define what customer service is. Customer service is about doing things right. It is about how you fix things that have gone wrong. It is also about doing things efficiently – to your customers' satisfaction – every time. A customer service programme must deal with:

- customer enquiries
- customer complaints
- quality issues
- invoicing and payment issues
- advice to customers
- faulty goods
- deliveries
- goods exchange and returns
- special requests.

If you look at this list and see a variety of problems that you habitually have to deal with, then it is almost certain that you have customer service problems and, if not addressed promptly and thoroughly, these will soon lead to a drop in profits – or will certainly result in an under-performing organisation. Let's look at how you can find out about your customer service issues.

Understanding what your customers want

As we discussed in Chapter 3, understanding who your customers are and why they buy from you is vital. When looking at customer service issues it is important to understand what will bring customer satisfaction – the holy grail of customer care. Do not think that the only people involved in customer care are those working in your customer service department or employed in an order-taking role. Almost everyone in any organisation can contribute to customer care and should be aware of this aspect of their role at all times. Let's look at the various types of roles that play a major part in customer care:

- **Customer-facing roles** – this will include salespeople, shop staff and management who may go out to see customers or see them when they visit the organisation's premises. This is the obvious group of people responsible for delivering a programme of customer care and should always receive training in this aspect of their jobs, and they should be selected for their expertise in this area.
- **Receptionists/telephone operatives** – must sound pleasant and efficient.
- **Order takers** – people working taking orders from customers must be efficient, helpful and friendly so that they make placing an order with your organisation a satisfactory experience for all customers. They must obviously have a depth of knowledge about the organisation's products and services.
- **Dispatch department** – people in the warehouse and dispatch department will not usually come into contact with your customers but how they do their jobs will undoubtedly have an effect on how your customers perceive the service your organisation gives them. If dispatch takes too long or the goods are poorly packed and arrive damaged then customers will notice and may well complain about poor service.
- **Production operatives** – the goods that are manufactured and supplied must comply with customer requirements. They will have standards to meet and their performance is key in meeting those standards.
- **Quality roles** – one essential element of customer satisfaction is supplying high-quality goods and services consistently. Everyone involved in production – including purchasing staff – will be involved in this but it is the

quality department that will ensure that quality standards are met so that the customer gets exactly what is expected, leading to customer satisfaction.

All the above roles must be carried out by trained personnel who have been made aware of the importance of keeping customers satisfied. There are many aspects of customer care.

- The efficiency, approachability and expertise of all staff.
- The prices on offer – value for money must be perceived by the customer.
- Reliability – your customers must know that they can trust your organisation to deliver what has been promised when required.
- Keeping customers informed – this might be when there has been a delay, for example. Sometimes it is not just what you do right for a customer but also how you put things right when things go wrong.
- Your organisation's order-to-delivery cycle – in most cases it is the quicker the better, so long delays in fulfilling orders may result in losing business.
- Your organisation's follow-up – you must have a system of following up on a regular basis to check that the customer is satisfied.
- The product or service – must meet the needs of your customers.

Some of these aspects of customer service are the responsibility of management, e.g. setting prices, but even in this case many others can contribute to management's understanding of customer requirements so that the correct decisions are made. Many other aspects can be put into practice by a variety of employees, so if all are made aware of the part they have to play in customer service, the greater will be the chance of satisfying customers on a regular basis.

Some tools to analyse situations and solve problems

There are two main areas of customer service that you must become familiar with in order to understand the specific problems your organisation may have with customer service – that represented by things that can be easily measured and the area that is less tangible which involves things such as employee attitudes and behaviour. The measurable aspects of customer service will show up in data such as:

- number of complaints
- value and number of credit notes issued
- repeat business rates
- number of days between receiving an order and delivering it.

All of these things can be shown in data that can be analysed and compared over time to see where problems may have developed. To analyse this sort of data you will have to keep the figures over a period of time so that valuable comparisons can be made. Is the number of complaints received in a month, for example, increasing or decreasing? To have success with this method you will need to ensure that:

- The data is reliable – this may require some reorganisation of your records and an overhaul of the database. This may seem like a lot of work – and in many organisations, if there has not been much attention to the record keeping process then it will take some time – but if your records are wrong then there is little point in using what they tell you to decide how to improve your business. You will be making a vast improvement simply by making sure your data is in order. A check of a typical database might reveal that, for example, 15 per cent of customers are lapsed or closed down and other entries duplicated.

● The data is consistent. Make sure that you are measuring things in the same way throughout. A careful check may reveal, for example, that a change in the way goods are packed mean that you are understating or overstating the number of units sold or that some products have been classified in different categories at different times.

● You are comparing like with like – comparing the number of complaints received in January with, for example, the number received in July will not give you a correct picture as you may not have a consistent number of complaints per month over the year – there may be peaks and troughs and these must be taken into account. Inconsistent figures however, can tell their own story. A peak should be investigated no matter when it happens.

This comparison of data that analyses aspects of customer service can be conducted as a one-off exercise to kick-start a programme of improvement or it can become a regular part of your job to keep an eye on these important indicators. Both regular and one-off exercises have their uses. Of course, the most important thing is to act on the information. Merely measuring something will not lead to improvement – you must make plans to change and put them into practice.

Many of the less tangible aspects of customer service can be discovered via customer feedback. This can provide you with detailed feedback about aspects such as:

● how your customers are being treated by your team
● salespeople's conduct when face-to-face with customers
● the quality of your telephone contact
● changes that customers would like to see
● what your customers like about your service

- complaints that a customer would not make unless contacted – some customers will not take the trouble to contact you and tell you what you are doing wrong but their discontent will eventually lead to your losing their business.

The less tangible aspects of customer service involve, as you can see, perceptions of your business and it is important that you obtain such information, analyse it and then use this information to improve your customer service. Using a system of customer feedback, you will also, if you ask the right questions, get information about what you are doing right as well as what is going wrong and this information can be just as valuable to you. If it's right, then you will want to do more of it and also, of course, to praise and reward the staff involved.

So, how will you get customer feedback? You can either get staff that are in contact with customers to obtain feedback on specific items or put together a written questionnaire that will be sent out to all customers, to ones that have been identified as important by your data, or to lapsed customers.

When designing a questionnaire remember that:

- You must have clear objectives – what do you want to find out?
- You must not allow customers to feel that the questionnaire is an imposition. Keep it short and to the point and, above all, make it quite clear that the aim is to improve customer service.
- A survey can collect data by post, email, telephone or in person.
- You should make it relevant and beneficial to your customers. Consider, in addition to an explanation of what you are trying to achieve, offering a place in a prize draw as an incentive to take part in the survey.

It is important to remember that customer feedback programmes, while an invaluable method of getting information from your customers, can also be a good way of passing information to them too.

Another valuable source of information about your organisation's performance in the area of customer service is your staff. How do they view the service they offer? How would they improve it? What resources do they need to be able to improve the service they offer? Finding out their perceptions can be very revealing.

One further way of getting a view of your customer service from outside your company is to use mystery shoppers. These are organisations offering a service whereby people pose as customers and compile reports about the quality of the service they have received. This can be carefully targeted so that the mystery shoppers ask just the right questions for you to find out what you need to know.

Thinking about changes

When you have found out where the problems are with your customer service you will need to find solutions. These problems could include:

- You have had complaints about how your employees deal with customers – if this is the case then you will need to review carefully the employees in question. If you have any doubt about how your customers are being treated by your employees, then a customer care training programme should be implemented.
- You have noted a high number of goods being returned as faulty – here you will need to review your quality procedures and production methods. The faults should first be analysed into broad categories such as manufacturing faults or damaged in transit, as well as

complaints of quantity deficiencies, incorrect goods sent
and so on.

● Your data shows a low rate of repeat orders – you may
be doing OK in getting new customers but having trouble
keeping them. Here you will need to decide whether the
problem is with the goods themselves or with the level of
customer care provided by your organisation. If you are
satisfied that your goods are of good quality and are as
described in your sales literature and by your
salespeople, and you do not have a problem with too
many goods returned, then you will need to look to your
customer care programme.

● You have had too many complaints about your after-
sales service – if this is the case you probably need to
ask your customers specific questions to find out exactly
what they expect in terms of after-sales. Is it more back-
up as to how to use or assemble the products? Or do
they want a quicker response from your service
engineers, for example?

● Taking too long to answer the telephone – are you sure
your telephone system is up to the job? Or are your
employees not aware of the need to respond promptly?

When you are sure that the customer service problems that your
research has identified have been dealt with, then you can go on to
think about other changes you could make to your customer care
programme that would make you stand out against other
organisations in your market area. Ideas you could consider include:

A customer loyalty programme

This can be part of a programme of incentives such as volume
discounts, small free items with a second order, discounts on
subsequent orders, entry into a prize draw with every order,

prompt payment discounts. For example, a coffee bar might give customers a card to be stamped on every visit and a free coffee offered for every tenth visit.

Additions to your website

Many businesses and individuals depend more and more on the internet for information about products. You could answer frequently asked questions (FAQs) on your website to save your customers having to contact you. If you decide to do this you must make sure that all existing customers are advised about the new service and that it is used as a selling point when approaching potential customers. You should decide on the information to be put on the website in consultation with your customers and those members of staff who have contact with customers, especially sales staff. By combining the information you can get from these sources, you will be sure to come up with genuinely useful additions to your website and information that will help to increase your sales and ensure customer satisfaction and loyalty.

Sales follow-ups

You could instigate a system of a courtesy call after each delivery to ensure that everything has gone according to your customers' expectations.

A customer contact programme

This is a regular, scheduled phone call, letter or email to customers to advise of developments in your organisation, special offers and so on. This must be handled with extreme care as unwanted calls can intensely annoy a busy person. However, if you can make sure that any calls you make are relevant and also potentially beneficial to the individual customer then this is a useful way of increasing sales via improved customer service. Each approach must be tailored to some extent to the individual customer. If you're making a special offer it should be linked to a previous purchase, for example. Amazon frequently carry this out by sending emails to existing customers recommending books or other products they may like to buy based on previous purchases – the latest book by an author whose work the customer has bought before, for example.

A customer help line

A free telephone number where customers can get advice about using your products can be a good selling point that will make customers feel safe about making the decision to buy from you. This, like everything else offered as an 'extra', must be done well. If people ring your customer help line and are kept hanging on the telephone then it can do your reputation more harm than good.

Evaluating changes

An integral part of any new system that you put into operation to improve performance must be a way of evaluating the success – or otherwise – of the changes made. To do this in the area of customer service you should first identify a number of Key Performance Indicators (KPIs) that, when measured, will indicate whether or not you are meeting targets and satisfying customers. KPIs should be quantifiable and measured as part of your normal processes. They should be closely linked to what you want to achieve. These KPIs could include:

- number of complaints received
- amount of goods returned as faulty or not as ordered
- length of the order-to-delivery cycle
- number of repeat orders received
- volume of orders received.

Make sure that you have considered your customers' requirements when setting the KPIs. The information you get from Key Performance Indicators should give you a picture of how satisfied your customers are with the service you are giving them. There are management information systems software products that you can buy that will do this measuring for you on a regular basis.

Of course, there are many areas of customer service that are not as easy to measure as the KPIs and in this case you will need to check your effectiveness in these areas by other means. For example, you can check satisfaction with a salesperson's conduct by getting feedback from customers. This qualitative evidence must be treated with care but can be very useful in helping you to see just what is going on and evaluating the success of the changes you have made. It is a very important part of your evaluation and should not be ignored merely because it is not as quantifiable. After all, what many improvements in customer service are aimed at is increasing customer satisfaction and this is a good way to find out if that is what you are getting from your changes.

Knowing when you need specialist help

You may feel, having done all your research, and having perhaps found that your problems with customer service in your organisation are too complicated to tackle internally, that you need to look outside your company for specialist help. This obviously needs careful thought. How do you decide what help you need and who might be available to help you? You may have come to the conclusion that you and your employees do not have the skills your business needs to improve its performance in the area of customer service. If you feel that you need help to resolve this one issue and that after that you will be able to do the job internally rather than needing help long-term to run the customer service department (when you would probably find it more cost-effective to recruit a permanent, experienced member of staff or to offer appropriate training to an existing employee) then you need to find a source of specialist help.

There is a wide variety of help available to businesses. Most of it has to be paid for and consultancy fees can seem very high to an organisation that is already worried about falling profits. However, there are some sources of free or reasonably priced specialist advice:

- **The Business Link organisation** – can offer different sorts of help (from general advice on their website, individual consultations for start-up businesses to very reasonably priced training) and can also put you in touch with other sources of help.
- **Local Chambers of Commerce** – similar advice and help as Business Link plus special offers and networking opportunities available if you become a member.
- **Professional bodies** – your own professional body or the body that represents people with the types of skills you are looking for may be able to offer useful advice about finding someone suitably qualified.
- **Trade associations** – if you are a member of a trade association you will have access to their list of people involved with work in your business area and will be able to verify their qualifications.
- **Local networking clubs** – attending these not only allow you to make contact with, and perhaps sell to or buy

from, local companies but also may get you some free advice from others in business.

If none of these sources of help for businesses seems to fit the bill in your case then you will need to decide whether you can pay for help and if so, how to choose the right adviser for your circumstances. Looking for help in a specific situation should not feel like an admission of failure. It is a fact that people working in a business are often too close to put problems right. They can see they have a problem but cannot see how time can be found for making change happen, how they would be able to change what is happening or how it should change. Someone coming in from outside the company should bring a dispassionate view, unclouded by set ideas about how the business has been run in the past. Here are the steps you should take if you are considering hiring an external consultant or adviser:

1. Set out a summary of the problem – back this up with the data you have accumulated and a brief description of your organisation including the number of employees, mission statement and values, what you do and what existing systems are in place.
2. Define what you are trying to achieve – are you trying to improve customer retention, to increase the skills your staff have, to implement a completely new customer care programme or to increase sales, for example?
3. Set objectives – as we've seen previously, objectives should always be SMART (Specific, Measurable, Achievable, Realistic and Time-based).
4. Decide on a budget – it is always a good idea to set a budget for work to be done. It is, of course, possible to approach consultants, tell them what the problem is and ask what can be done for that amount but that may result in overspending.

5. Ask around – many businesses find advisers and consultants to work with by recommendation. If a business similar to yours has had success working with a certain adviser then it is well worth considering whether that consultant would be right for you too.

When looking for someone to work with look for:

- Someone who has experience in your industry – find out about projects they have worked on.
- Someone who has worked with organisations of your size – if you are a small company with just a few employees and a small budget, a consultant who usually works with large multinational organisations will probably not be suitable for you.
- Someone who can demonstrate experience of solving problems like yours – ask them about their views on customer service and how they have helped other organisations with similar issues. Can they give you references from previous projects? If so, check them out and if not, proceed cautiously.
- Someone who is suitably qualified and/or is a member of a professional body.

When you have found the right person to help with your customer service issues then you will need to ensure that your relationship is put on the correct footing right from the start. In addition to a clear definition of what you are trying to achieve and what the problems are, you will to need develop a work plan with your new adviser with targets set throughout the life of the project. This will help you to identify problems if they occur by comparing the goals set with the progress to date. Any organisation employing the services of a professional agency or consultant must play a part in achieving results. It is not possible to hand over the problem and sit back, so constant communication is essential with regular review meetings a prominent feature of the relationship. If you sense problems in the relationship – a lack of communication, for example, or limited progress towards your goals – then the sooner it is sorted out the better. Of course, the problem may be caused by you or someone in the organisation. As all external advisers have to rely on what they are told and on getting cooperation from their clients, ask the adviser what the problem is and help them to resolve it. If all else fails you may need to end the relationship but that is usually a better option than persevering with something that is expensive and is not working.

This short section on getting external help to resolve a problem with customer service should help you to decide whether you need such help and to choose a consultant or adviser. Drawing up a contract and working with people outside your organisation is, however, a specialist subject outside the scope of this book. External advice can be expensive and risky and you must be clear, before you enter into any contract, just what you need and that the consultant also fully understands and agrees with what you need. If you can come to this agreement, agree mutually acceptable terms – including when and how charges are to be paid, what additional expenses are to be paid by you and who will do the work (you and your staff or the consultant and his or her staff) – then you have a chance of a successful relationship and a satisfactory outcome.

SUMMARY

This chapter was all about spotting when you have problems with customer service and then looking at how you can find solutions. We examined possible problem areas that would signal to you that your organisation's customer service is letting it down. The keys to solving these problems include a thorough understanding of what your customers want and the acknowledgement that customer service should be the responsibility of everyone in the organisation rather than just the sales department or people with customer-facing roles, and also an appreciation of the various aspects of customer care.

We then went on to look at how you could analyse the problem and come up with a solution, taking into account data about tangible aspects of customer care such as the number of complaints received and also the less tangible aspects such as customer perceptions. We discussed the need for reliable, consistent data and also how to get effective feedback from customers so that the specific problems that have been identified can be solved.

Following resolution of the issues identified, extra aspects of customer service can be instigated that would constitute a customer care programme, including a customer help line, customer-friendly changes to the website, a customer contact programme and other changes aimed at helping customers.

An examination of how to evaluate the results of these changes in customer care followed, with an explanation of Key Performance Indicators (KPIs) that could be used in this respect.

Finally, we looked at when you should get specialist help. First, we considered the sources of help available, including Chambers of Commerce, trade associations and networking. Then we went on to consider engaging a consultant who could analyse the problems and instigate a programme of customer care throughout the organisation. The importance of thorough preparation before approaching an outside source of help was emphasised to ensure that you are clear about what the problem is and what you are trying to achieve.

ACTION CHECKLIST

1. Find out what is the average number of complaints received per month from customers in your organisation. Is every complaint logged? If not, you may have to do some extra detective work, approaching a number of departments to get their take on the problem.

2. Find out how each type of complaint is resolved. For example, if goods are returned are they automatically replaced? What investigation is carried out?

3. What is the value of invoices currently under query? Do you think there is a problem with this aspect of customer care? How long, on average, do invoices remain under query?

4. If your organisation does not already have a set of KPIs that they are working to, what do you think would be three useful ones to set? If there are already KPIs in use, can you think of three more that would improve customer service?

5. Can you think of one aspect of customer care that is not currently in use in your organisation that could be a useful addition?

06

How can you improve customer service?

As we have already seen, customer service affects the bottom line so it is vital that you get it right. It can improve profitability, increase your sales and help to build a good reputation for your organisation. It is not too difficult to improve customer service but it does require commitment from everyone in the business. It is not just the salespeople's job or the responsibility of the Customer Service Department. Customer care can be affected by every employee including production and dispatch personnel, quality control staff and all of the management team. Your first challenge in improving customer service in your organisation might well be to convince some people of its importance and of the part they play. Also, unless your senior managers and finance people are committed to it you will have to sell the benefits of improving customer service to them as, inevitably, improvements will require their support to push changes through the company and to access the resources they control.

Key management challenges in improving customer service

If you already have the support of senior management to improve customer service, then the main challenge is in finding out where you are going wrong. As we discussed in the previous chapter, this can involve a great deal of research and analysis. It may be that you have a 'gut feeling' about what is going wrong – and you may well be correct – but nevertheless you should do the work to ascertain exactly what the problem is. Properly carried out, such research should give you a complete picture and may reveal problems you did not suspect were there. You will need to gather as much detail as possible on all areas of customer service such as complaints, returned goods, invoicing errors, technical queries, customer feedback and, of course, statistics about your organisation's performance in areas such as length of delivery period, number of rings before telephones are answered and so on.

If, on the other hand, you do not have the support of senior management and others in your organisation for the need to improve customer service, then your challenge will be to sell the idea – and the benefits of customer service improvements – to them. You will need to make a business case that demonstrates the advantages to be gained by making customer service a priority in the organisation. This must be as specific as possible in terms of the financial gains to be made so you will have to choose areas for improvement where the gains can be quantified and where you will easily be able to demonstrate success. So, for example, you may choose to concentrate on increasing sales from existing customers. If this is where you start, don't forget to point out, as part of your business case, that sales from existing customers are far more cost effective than trying to get sales from new customers with all the initial expenses they bring such as increased number of sales visits necessary, setting up accounts and so on. Existing customers are already set up on your internal systems, they have a payment record with you so, hopefully, you know that they will pay your invoices and, most importantly, they have already selected your organisation as a supplier.

We have looked in earlier chapters at several ways of retaining existing customers and how customer service improvements can increase sales from existing customers. Later, in Chapter 10, we will also look at how to gain new customers so all that remains in this area is regaining lost customers to complete the picture. Like existing customers, old customers once chose your organisation as a supplier but there is a disadvantage in that there is some reason why they stopped buying from you. The first thing you need to do, therefore, is to find out why this was. Did they stop buying from you because:

● your prices were too high?
● another organisation offered them something you weren't giving them?
● your customer service was unsatisfactory?
● they no longer needed your product?

If the answer you come up with is one of the first three suggestions, then you should investigate further to see if you can regain this customer. If it is the last option and you are certain that they still have no need for what you are offering, then you can put that customer to one side with no further action required.

So, how can you get a customer back? First you must re-establish regular contact with the customer. Don't let them feel neglected, send them a newsletter, ring and check if there is anything they need, try to make an appointment to see them, advise them of any new developments, such as new products or improvements to your customer service. Your next step will be to put right what went wrong when they bought from you in the past. If they received an offer from one of your competitors, see if you can match it. This may mean looking carefully at your prices and costs to make sure that regaining the business would be worthwhile for you. Before offering any reduction in price though, do make sure that what they are currently buying is very similar to what you supply. It may be that they have settled for a lower quality product in order to get the price reduction. If the problem was concerned with your customer service, you will have to find out exactly what the problem was then work out a way that you can meet this customer's requirements. Regaining lost customers can be very satisfying and good for business but judgement must be used to determine whether the customer is unlikely to return to your organisation and when to stop investing time and money in the attempt to regain them.

Now that we've dealt with retaining and regaining customers, sometimes using improved customer service to assist in the exercise, let's look at the solutions you may choose to solve specific customer service problems.

Choosing your solution to a customer service problem

The solution you choose to any problem depends, of course, on what you have decided the problem is. There is one thing you can do, however, that will almost always help: training. If you are not totally confident that all staff involved in customer service (and, as we have already seen, that means almost all staff) have been trained so that they understand exactly how their roles and behaviour affect the customer's perception of the organisation, then putting into place a programme of training for everyone will produce benefits. We will look at customer service training in a bit more detail later in this chapter.

However, apart from training, there is a variety of solutions to the different customer service issues. There are many aspects of customer service – and they can all go wrong. Let's look at them one by one to see what solutions might be appropriate for each one.

Returned goods

If you have a high returns rate then you need to analyse the reasons for the returns. Are the goods faulty or of poor quality? Are they not living up to customers' expectations? Have you sent the wrong goods? Many of these problems can be resolved by changes to the product or working practices and/or enforcement of a rigorous quality system including a pre-dispatch check. Don't forget that often it is not the mistakes we make in business but how we put those mistakes right. A prompt phone call to a customer to apologise, find out what the problem is and a promise to put it right immediately (and doing so, of course!) is often all that is needed, so if you have problems in this area make sure that you designate a member of staff responsible for this.

Technical enquiries

Many products these days are highly complicated and need some explanation to customers. You will need to tackle this on two fronts. Firstly, in supplying top-quality, easily understandable literature with each product so that every customer has the information they need to be able to install and use the product as intended. It is advisable to get professional help in producing this sort of literature. Not only does this require someone who fully understands the product and how it works, but it should also be written by someone who understands customers and has good writing skills so that you do not get a document that is too technical and full of jargon. Secondly, you need to be sure that you have a technical department that is easily accessible to your customers. Depending on your type of product you may need to set up a specialised helpdesk for this purpose. Don't forget training in dealing with customers when you're setting up anything like this.

Invoicing

At first glance this seems like a problem for the invoicing department. However, mistakes made on the order, at the sales stage or at the order entry stage, will all result in incorrect prices showing on the invoice. Finding out the root of the problem will show you where extra checks need to be made. Prompt resolution of invoicing problems will not only impress your customers but it will also improve your cash flow. If invoice queries are neglected then the invoices will not be paid – and unpaid invoices in any quantity are a disaster for any business.

Communication

If you receive a complaint from a customer regarding how they have been spoken to by one of your team then immediate action must be taken. Of course, you will need to find out the employee's version of events, but even if you suspect that the customer may be being unreasonable there is still a problem to be resolved. First, an apology – regardless of blame – must be given to the customer and then training of the employee and possibly others in the department must be arranged. Efficient and pleasant communication with customers is of paramount importance.

Queries

Here you will need to analyse what the queries are about. Are they about technical aspects of the products? If so, look back at the earlier point in this section about technical enquiries. If they are price queries about existing orders and invoices then you will need to check that the level of accuracy set down in your quality standards is being met and, if it isn't, you may need to put in place further checks. Also, if this is found to be a problem, make sure that your quotations are crystal clear so that there can be no doubt about the price to be paid.

Delivery

The warehousing and dispatch departments are the last time the company will handle the goods before they arrive with the customer and problems here will soon become apparent in terms of complaints from customers. If the late delivery is due to problems in production then the dispatch department must always highlight the problem to management, so make sure a system is in place for this to happen on a routine basis.

Too few repeat orders

Do customers order once and then go somewhere else for their next supply of that product? Your analysis of order patterns should show this up and it may take a great deal of research such as contacting those customers who have ordered only once from you to ascertain their reasons. Take careful note of what these customers tell you as this can be a major pointer to problems in customer service or in the quality of the product you are supplying.

Who will help to improve customer service?

There are three correct answers to this question:

1. Your team – if customer service is your area of responsibility then the people you work closely with will be the most important people in delivering improvements to your organisation's customer service. We will look more closely at working with a team to improve customer service in the next section.

2. Everyone in your organisation – as we have seen previously everyone in an organisation must play their part in the provision of good customer service. This ranges from the sales department contacting the customer before the order comes in, to the order receipt department presenting an efficient and pleasant face of your business to the customer, to the production department supplying the correct goods on time, to the quality department making sufficient checks, to the dispatch department getting the goods out on time, to the invoicing department sending a prompt, correct invoice. And, as we have seen previously, the commitment from management – along with the resources to make satisfactory customer service happen – must be in place.

3. Your customers – the feedback you get from customers is invaluable in improving service. You may choose to send out a formal questionnaire to many customers to elicit their responses about the level of your organisation's customer service and this can often form the basis of your decision as to where improvements need to be made. However, do not look upon this as a one-off exercise. Getting customer feedback should be

an ongoing process. Don't forget that for feedback to be useful, someone has to act on it.

Working with a team to improve customer service

Having obtained feedback from customers to help you decide where improvements are necessary, gained the approval and commitment of senior managers to your customer service improvement plans and liaised with other departments within your organisation to do their bit towards resolving specific problems – for example quality or delivery issues – the main thrust of the day-to-day business of improving customer service usually falls to one department.

As mentioned previously, one of the most important aspects that will contribute to the running of an efficient and effective customer service department is the training that members of the department receive. There is a school of thought that training is always 'a good thing', but in business it must be seen to enhance the performance of your organisation. It is always necessary to analyse the skills needs of your department and match these needs to the skills that the members of your team possess. It is only when you know what skills you need and exactly where the gaps exist that you can make meaningful decisions about training requirements. When you can see clearly what skills you need your team to acquire you will then need to consider what sort of training can fill that gap. This could include:

- **The level of training needed** – there is little business sense in someone who needs to be able to take orders from customers over the phone being sent on a Masters degree course in sales (unless, of course, you think there is great potential there) as it won't fill your immediate business need. There are courses and other types of training available at all levels so choose carefully.

- **One-to-one** – this used to be called 'sitting with Nellie' and so may be thought old-fashioned, but it is still a very useful way of sharing skills within your team. If you have someone who is extremely proficient – and who you think is capable of passing on their skills – then pairing them with someone who needs to improve skills in that area can be a very cost-effective method of training.
- **Mentoring or buddying** – mentoring is a more formal arrangement where an employee receives advice from a more senior colleague and can go to them for help. Buddying is where two colleagues – who may or may not work in the same department – are paired up. This is often useful for a new member of staff learning their way around an organisation.
- **Work-based assignments** – this method can be used to improve a variety of skills. Not only can it be used to ensure that the employee has to examine a particular topic in some detail but it can also give practice in preparing a written report, presentational skills and analytical skills. There are also often business benefits from the results of the projects if they are carefully targeted. So, for example, a work-based project to look at ways to reduce costs may produce good ideas and real savings.
- **Distance learning** – there is an enormous choice of subjects that can be studied in this way. This can range from literacy and numeracy to basic computer use or a degree. This type of training can have a major benefit for a business, particularly if the team is small, in that employees do not need to be away from the workplace for long periods in order to complete a course of training.
- **External courses** – this is usually what is thought of when training is mentioned. These can last a day or two

when a very specific topic is to be covered or may need an ongoing commitment of several years for a more general or higher level course.

Having chosen a training delivery method and level, your next step will be to find a suitable training provider. Recommendations from fellow business people are always worth checking out or you can get advice from colleges, Chambers of Commerce, trade associations and organisations such as Business Link or Train to Gain. You will need to conduct a bit of research into the various training providers who are able to offer the sort of training you're looking for. Check out the following:

- Appropriateness of the course – will it fulfil your need?
- Experience – have the people delivering the training got plenty of experience in training in general and in the specific subject?
- Qualifications – is the trainer suitably qualified?
- Value for money – could you get the same result at a lower price?
- Duration and intensity – is the length of the course justified and will the intensity of the course be right for the person receiving the training?
- Testimonials – does the training provider have testimonials available? Speaking to people who have actually received training from the provider can be really useful.

Whatever method of training you decide suits your purpose, it will be necessary to evaluate its effectiveness as a matter of routine. A questionnaire sent to the trainee after they have received training can ascertain the effectiveness by checking how the trainee rates the course and the tutor. This could include an assessment of the methods and resources used, the venue, how much they think they have learned and the skills displayed by the tutors. You should also ask how what they have learned can be used in their day-to-day work. Training your staff is an investment in your business and, like any investment, you must get a positive result. What you find out following any training that you arrange for your employees should be used to inform your training decisions in the future.

Of course, when you evaluate the skills that your team possesses you may find that you have all the skills you need within your team. However, even if this is the case, you may feel that improvements are still possible. It may be that you need to redistribute tasks and responsibilities within your team to make the most of the skills each member has.

There are a number of leadership skills necessary to manage a team to improve customer service within an organisation, so you should not neglect your own training. If you need to brush up your motivational and leadership skills, then arrange appropriate training as soon as practically possible. Getting everyone to work together as a team is of vital importance. Consider the following:

- Everyone must know where you're going and how you're going to get there. Make your goals and objectives clear to your team from the beginning and keep them updated as the situation changes.
- Communication with your team and within your team is essential. Set the systems in place so that this happens continually and everyone is kept informed. Remember that communication is two-way. Make sure your team members feel free to give their input and that there is a clear and easy way for them to do this.
- Teams work best when the members feel a loyalty to one another so try to engender the 'team spirit' whenever possible.
- Make sure everyone knows what their responsibilities are and what part they play in achieving the aims of the department.

- How you treat your team members will affect their performance. You should show that you trust them rather than continually looking over their shoulders, treat them with respect and show them encouragement to do a good job.
- Try to make sure that each member of the team has a measure of job satisfaction as this leads to greater productivity. This can be difficult in the case of very routine jobs, but everyone can take pride in a job well done and it is your job to lead your team to be able to see when this is the case.
- Hold short but effective meetings. If you plan exactly what a meeting is meant to achieve and set time limits for it then you should avoid the boring, unproductive meetings that occur in many organisations. It can be helpful to split the meeting into five or ten minute slots and make the rule that no agenda item should last for more than this. A possible alternative that some organisations use to keep control of the unproductive chat that goes on in most meetings is to hold them standing up. Remember that no efficiently run meeting would be complete without a list of action points, allocated to the appropriate person and with a time limit for action included.
- Encourage innovation. Meetings held with your team specifically to generate ideas for possible improvements can be hugely successful and will, of course, make team members feel that they are a valuable part of the organisation. Get the team together, without interruptions, and explain what you are trying to do, then give them free rein to brainstorm ideas. It is best not to comment too much at this stage about the value of the ideas – just get the ideas out. It is important to ensure that everyone is given the opportunity to contribute –

remember that some people will not be as vocal and forceful as others but that does not mean that their ideas won't be just as useful.

● Reward good work and initiative. The rewards do not have to be large – sometimes simple recognition of good work and effort is enough. There are a number of types of reward schemes such as 'Employee of the Month' awards, a bonus scheme (closely linked to results), staff outings, time off when targets are reached and so on. The most important thing is to ensure the reward is seen as fair and transparent. Reward systems should be 'out in the open' as this is the way they have the best effect on the motivation of the team.

Communicating with customers about changes

The method (letter, fax, email, telephone or face-to-face) we use to communicate with customers about changes in customer service procedures may depend on the extent of the changes. If it is a minor change then a quick telephone call may suffice. However, for anything more than small adjustments to procedures, it is advisable to use more than one method. This is because this communication must meet several requirements. It must:

● convey the information about the nature of the change
● check – and record – reaction to the change
● ensure that sufficient time for taking in the information is allowed – this is sometimes not possible during a telephone call
● sell the benefits of the change to the customer
● retain the customer's business.

A combination of methods of communication is preferable, for example a phone call followed up by a letter, will help to ensure that all the above criteria are met. If a letter is sent out simply explaining the changes then it is likely that in the absence of a follow-up telephone call a misunderstanding could go unnoticed or that the full benefits of the changes are not explained clearly.

While communicating with customers about specific changes in customer service matters, it is important also to convey the message that the organisation considers customer service to be of prime importance. If the positive changes that the organisation is implementing are to be used to their full potential then the benefits that they can bring to customers must also be sold by fully communicating them to customers. Unless the benefits of changes are sold to customers then some customers may view them as merely changes that disrupt the way things have been done in the past rather than appreciating that they can gain from them.

Monitoring performance

If you have monitored the results of changes to systems in terms of KPIs (see Chapter 5) as you have made them, then at this stage you will need to look at the performance in terms of how it has affected your customers and how it has affected your staff. Measurement and comparison of your KPIs before and after the changes will tell you how your results have changed and whether specific goals have been met. Just as important is to check what your customers and your staff think about the changes.

You must find out if customers are more satisfied now than they were before the changes took place and the only reliable way of doing this is to ask them. A straightforward question such as, 'How have the changes affected you?' will do the job and should be part of the routine follow-up by sales and customer service staff to customers who they made aware of the changes at the beginning of the project. It is important that the responses are recorded. You should then be able to quantify the success – or otherwise – of the changes in terms of a percentage satisfied. Of course, if any customers say they have been adversely affected then it is imperative that further discussions take place and the appropriate adjustments made.

In terms of how the changes have affected employees, you need to find out about any problems that staff have encountered so that any necessary adjustments to ways of working, software and so on can be made. A major benefit of improved customer service is that staff morale is improved and continually reviewing the effect of your changes on employees can further this process dramatically. The best way to go about this – especially where a small number of employees are involved – is to hold individual interviews or informal chats about how they see the changes and to get their ideas on taking the improvements further. If this is not possible because of the large numbers involved, then either conduct a written/email survey to get this information or break the teams down into more manageable numbers and elect a spokesperson for each small team.

It is important to remember that improvements to customer service are not just about KPIs but involve people's opinions and feelings and these can be just as valid as any quantifiable target. To have maximum benefit this process must be ongoing and not conducted as a one-off exercise.

SUMMARY

This chapter concentrated on how to improve customer service. We looked at the different problems you may encounter that are affecting your organisation's customer service, such as customer complaints, invoice queries, too many technical queries, delivery problems and a lack of repeat orders. Then we examined the possible solutions to each of those problems.

Next we looked at who will help to solve customer service problems – your team, your customers and everyone in your organisation. In particular we examined how you could work with a team to resolve customer service problems. The main skills needed when working with a team are those of being able to motivate and lead and, when reviewing training skills for the whole team responsible for improving customer service, the manager must make sure that they do not neglect their own training needs in this area. We discussed how to assess what training might be necessary, what sorts of training solutions are available and how to choose the right solution to any problems identified.

Having decided to make changes to improve customer service it is important to inform your customers about the changes. They must not be allowed to see any changes as an irritation or of no consequence to them but staff need to impart the information not only about the practical details of the changes but also the rationale behind them. There is a need for the benefits of the changes to be 'sold' to customers and the ultimate aim must be to satisfy and retain customers.

Finally we looked at how we can monitor performance following the implementation of changes necessary to improve customer service. Obviously, Key Performance Indicators are the ideal way of keeping a check on how the changes have affected sales figures and such things as the number of complaints received or quantity of goods returned, but there should also be an awareness of less tangible effects, for example how customers have reacted and how staff have been affected. This can only be done effectively by asking customers and staff by way of phone calls, letters and surveys in the case of customers; and by meetings, surveys or interviews to find out staff views.

ACTION CHECKLIST

1. Look again at the list of types problems that can occur in customer service. Which of these do you think affects your organisation most?

2. Now choose two possible solutions to the problem you have identified and think about whether these would overcome the problem.

3. Write a list of your own good points and bad points in terms of leadership and motivational skills so that you are in a position to assess your own training needs in these areas.

4. Think about the last change to customer service delivery that was made in your organisation and find out how it was communicated to customers. Do you think this was satisfactory?

5. What effect do you think changes to customer service systems could have on staff?

07

How can you be sure customers are satisfied?

Managing delivery of customer service

As we have said previously, it is not just sales staff that are involved in customer service, it involves the whole organisation. The business should be run so that customer service is given high priority. This means that an organisation-wide approach must be taken. Most businesses are structured by function – there are departments for production, sales, quality, accounts, warehousing and dispatch, customer service and so on, but all these departments must be made to work together with a focus on customer satisfaction. This requires a different approach to management and it is worth looking at a definition of management here to understand the way this can be done. Management can be said to be 'getting things done through other people'. Taking that as a starting point, it does not matter too much if a manager of a quality department, for example, has specialist knowledge of quality control and the production methods (this knowledge will often be acquired on the job anyway by a sufficiently enthusiastic manager) as it is far more important for him or her to possess management skills and to be able to use them to ensure customer satisfaction. Teamwork is important – each of the individual team members may not possess all the skills necessary but if the team can be made to work well together a lot can be achieved. This more flexible management approach is becoming increasingly popular as the emphasis is placed more and more on customer service.

Case study

How complaints are dealt with is a very important aspect of customer service and could make the difference between losing and retaining a customer. As individuals we will all have experience as a customer every day and should take note of how we are treated – who is getting it right, and how? For example, a supermarket shopper complained about the quality of some fruit she had bought and was treated dismissively by the customer service staff, so she wrote a letter to the store's manager. A response arrived a couple of weeks later which was again unsatisfactory. The letter said 'we are sorry you were not satisfied', rather than 'we are sorry we got it wrong'. She has not visited that store since. She also had occasion to complain to her broadband supplier and received a prompt, multi-departmental response. Someone from the technical department called her and got her back online, then the same person called again the next day to check everything was sorted out to her satisfaction. This was followed up by a letter from the Customer Service Manager apologising for the shortcomings and assuring her that the error had now been corrected and lessons learned. This consumer had been considering changing her broadband supplier but, because of their prompt and comprehensive response, is now a loyal customer.

The lessons to be learned from these two examples are clear:

- If you got it wrong, say so and apologise.
- Tell the customer what you will do to put things right – and do it.
- Follow up any problem until the customer is satisfied.
- Involve anyone necessary in the organisation to reach a solution to the problem.
- Keep the customer informed.
- Use complaints as an opportunity to satisfy a customer.

Setting clear standards

All the different elements of customer service must be assessed and standards set as to how each aspect should be handled. Clear standards will ensure not only that staff know what is expected of them in specific circumstances but also that a consistent approach is adopted throughout the customer service process. Let's look at these different elements and how standards could be set.

Initial contact

There is a delicate balance to be met here so that customers who contact the organisation feel that they have been helped in a friendly and efficient manner without being annoyed by high-pressure sales tactics. Of course, sales staff will want to get the order but it is important to deal with the customer in a tactful way so that they do not feel intimidated. Remember that first impressions count – and can last for some time – so standards for the initial contact are important. The standards to be set depend upon the type of contact, so, for example, telephone enquiries should be answered in a certain number of rings, letters to be answered the same day they are received and so on. Standard replies can be formulated, for example the offer to send out full information or to ring back with information within a set time. The degree of formality with which customers are dealt can also be subject to a standard.

Product information

Full information must be readily available to anyone who is dealing with customers. This may include technical specifications, prices, warranties and availability as well as information about the organisation's terms and conditions including payment terms. Both written and verbal responses to queries should be clear and unambiguous. There should be no 'hidden extras' anywhere in your customer service process. It should be clear what is and is not included. Staff training may be necessary in order to bring product and organisational knowledge up to the standard required.

Ordering procedure

This should be simple and straightforward but comprehensive. As always in devising procedures to deal with customers, the customer should be at the centre. So, the order process should not include long, complicated forms designed to suit the organisation's systems but should be short and clear so that the customer can place an order easily. The customer should be in no doubt as to what details are required and they should not be required to supply superfluous information. Follow-up order acknowledgement should also be clear and straightforward and must be sent promptly, stating what the order is for and when it will be delivered.

Delivery

Honesty is always the best policy when advising delivery times. It is far worse to promise a date then let the customer down than to agree a realistic date at the outset. Targets can be set to limit the number of orders that are dispatched later than promised and also on the time taken between receipt and dispatch of order. Another aspect of delivery that can affect customer service is damage or loss in transit. This should be monitored to ensure customers are not having to sort out these problems and getting a bad impression of your organisation.

Invoicing

These must be clear and always sent out promptly. You may want to set standards based on the number of invoice queries you receive with a programme of continual improvement alongside the goal of reducing the number of errors. Incorrect invoices are an irritation to customers so will have an obvious impact on their perception of your customer service levels. Another point to note here – accounts staff who take invoice queries are part of your customer service team so make sure that they have had the appropriate training in dealing with customers.

After-sales service

Just because the product has been delivered and the customer has paid the invoice, this does not mean that the customer service department's job is complete. After-sales service can take various forms. It could involve anything from assembling the product (in the case of complicated machinery) or training the customer's staff in its use, to a card included with the product that aims at obtaining customer's impressions of the product upon receipt. It should not be forgotten that instruction manuals and product literature that may be included with the delivery of the product are also part of the customer service and will have a negative impact on the customer's impression of the company if badly written or produced. In any event, a programme of follow-up calls can be instigated and targets can be set for how and when these are carried out.

Staff attitudes and behaviour

This aspect of customer service, being less tangible and quantifiable than other aspects, can be more difficult to set standards for. However, enormous improvements can be made in the quality of customer service by the use of a few simple measures to train staff and develop the right attitudes. As we discussed in the previous section in this chapter, it is important to note that all staff can make a contribution to customer service and it is management's job to ensure that standards are set and adhered to.

Customer surveys

Asking your customers what they think of your customer service is one of the most reliable ways of checking the level of satisfaction.

However, a customer survey must be done correctly to ensure meaningful results. It is important to keep it simple and you should consider the following:

- Who will you ask? You may be tempted to send out a written survey to every one of your customers but this can be a very expensive and unmanageable option. If you want to survey your entire customer base, and your budget allows for it, then it may be advisable to use an external research agency to do this. If, however, you need to control costs and want to handle the survey yourself you will need to limit the number of surveys you send out – up to maybe a few hundred or so – and then spread them evenly throughout your customer base. Alternatively, you could limit the number of surveys you send out and select customers from each segment of your customer base. So, for example, you may have segmented your customer base by the value of orders they place or by the size of their organisation and you would survey a few in each segment.
- What form will the survey take? Most surveys are paper-based but email is becoming increasingly popular as it is a cost-effective way of contacting large numbers of people. You may also find a survey placed on your website – together with an appropriate incentive to complete the survey online – will be productive. These can even be made to appear automatically when a website page is opened, thereby increasing the response rate.
- How will you get it to your customers? You may simply post a written survey form out to the customers you have selected for the survey or you may find that a response card included with goods sent out or with invoices is convenient and successful.

- Make sure you include with the survey an explanation of what you are trying to do and a polite invitation to take part.
- You may wish to consider offering an incentive to improve the response rate. This could take the form of a reduction on products to be ordered in the future, entry into a prize draw or a discount coupon.

When you have decided on these basics about your survey, you can turn your attention to the actual questions:

- Keep it short – both the overall length of the questionnaire and the questions themselves should be kept short and to the point. Don't try to be too clever with the questions as anything that confuses or irritates customers cannot produce the right results. If the questions are too long or complicated then it is unlikely that you will get a high response rate. Questionnaires should normally only take a few minutes to complete. If you believe that the information you need justifies anything longer, then it would be advisable to engage the services of a research company with extensive experience of how to handle surveys to get meaningful responses without upsetting customers.
- Make them unambiguous – be straightforward and ask yourself each question. Is there any other way of interpreting it than that which you intended? Use simple language.
- Keep response options to a minimum – but make sure that you have covered the range of responses that you may get. You must be sure that you are not leading the respondent to give the answer that you want to hear. The easiest of responses is a box to tick where the answer is yes or no but if you want to get relative responses then

devise an easy to understand scale – such as strongly agree, agree, don't know, disagree and strongly disagree – with a maximum of five points on it.

- When you are designing the questionnaire remember that you – or someone in your team – will have to analyse the results. For this reason it is preferable to use closed questions, for example, 'Would you buy this product again?' This way you will get a limited number of different responses to your questions and you will be able to group the responses for analysis.

- Have a trial run – either get someone in your organisation who has not been involved with the survey to give you their opinion about the effectiveness and clarity of the questionnaire or, if you are particularly close to one customer, you may wish to let them look at it. Be open to suggestions – it is easy to become so involved in a project that you are unable to see its faults.

When you are satisfied that the questionnaire is as short and simple as you can make it, get it out to your selected recipients and wait for the responses. When you've received sufficient responses you will need to analyse them. Again, you must keep this process as simple as possible. What you are aiming at is percentage responses and it should not be a complicated matter to count the positive and negative answers and record them as percentages of the total responses received. You should also record your response rate. At this point you will probably be required to produce a report detailing the results of the survey and outlining your plans to use what you have found to change the way you deal with customers. You may also be required to quantify the improvements that you can make.

Keeping in touch with customers

There are several ways of keeping in contact with customers:

Advertising

This may be the first 'contact' your potential customer has with your organisation so it must be effective and well-positioned. Look out for different advertising outlets by analysing what your customers are reading and viewing. If your customers are unlikely to be heavy internet users (although this is becoming less and less likely) then there would be little point in advertising exclusively online. If most of your business is done locally then, local radio stations and local magazines and directories will suit your purpose and can be a very cost-effective. If, on the other hand, you have a national or international customer base then you will have to spread your net wider – but will probably have the budget to do this.

Marketing materials

If you're sending anything out to your customers it should be of good quality and a positive representation of your organisation. This applies to all forms of marketing, including your website, contact by email and letter or by regular newsletters.

Salespeople

This is the most obvious point of contact that an organisation has with its customers and a regular programme of visits and/or telephone calls should be in place. Remember that this is a two-way process and that not only can you impart information about your goods or services to your customers but that they can also give you valuable information about your levels of customer service, what products they may like to buy in the future, what your competitors are offering, how the market is going and so on. Although in many organisations the salespeople are very good at getting this information out of their customers, some are not so good at disseminating the information. There should be a system in place so that if a customer has a complaint, however small, it is registered and then must follow a set path until it is resolved. Of course, one of the last steps in this process must be a call to the customer to check that they are satisfied with the outcome. This call will not only bring the complaints process to a conclusion, it will also show your customer that their complaint has been taken seriously. Too many complaints are dealt with internally but the customer who complained is not kept informed. This is inadequate customer service.

Training is an important aspect in this situation. Salespeople who are customer-facing need to be made aware of how the system works within the organisation so that they feed the correct information into the system and the people dealing with the complaint must be trained in how to deal with both their internal contacts to resolve the complaint and also how to present the information about the resolution of the problem to the customer.

The media

Local and national newspapers and magazines, television broadcasters and radio stations all deal with 'news' fed to them by businesses on their own behalf or by public relations (PR) companies. This could be as simple as a new product launch or a piece when a long-serving employee retires, or something financial fed to the business sections of newspapers. There are lots of opportunities for organisations to get some publicity of this kind and done properly it can position your products or services in a specific context. An example of this would be if you could get your new organic face cream mentioned in an article in one of the more upmarket women's magazines.

Financial

People working in the financial departments of the organisation will need to contact customers. This may be to send out invoices or to chase up overdue payments. These staff should, of course, be trained in how to deal with customers and when you're sending out invoices, reminders and statements you should consider using it as an opportunity to send marketing materials, special offers and so on.

Complaints

This is another form of customer contact and you should have systems in place to ensure that complaints are dealt with promptly and effectively. Although a lot of customer contact in the complaints department will be responding to customers it can also be made to be proactive by telephoning customers – on a regular basis or following the resolution of a complaint – to check that everything is OK.

Customer contact programmes

Some companies find that having specific intervals between routine calls to customers pays dividends. This could take the form of a routine call to take an order, a call when new products are launched, calls to announce special offers or simply a call that is friendly and presented as 'just keeping in touch'. All of these types of call need very delicate handling if they are not to be viewed as a nuisance by customers and the interval between calls, which will vary for the different types of call, should be carefully calculated. However, they are an important part of any customer care programme.

Getting your marketing mix right can be a question of trial and error but thorough research and a comprehensive knowledge of your customers' requirements will increase your chances of success. All of the methods of keeping in touch with your customers can be part of your marketing mix and what you include and how much emphasis you put on each element will depend on what your research shows. Let's look at how one business reviewed and changed their marketing strategy:

Case study

The first step for a firm of recruitment consultants who wanted to improve their marketing was to conduct a review of the organisation's strengths and weaknesses. This involved an examination of the whole business, a survey of its top 100 customers and extensive market research. A great deal of information was gained from this and it took some weeks to filter out what was useful and then to decide what action to take. The main findings were that there was little awareness of the organisation in the marketplace but that their customers were extremely pleased with the service they received. They also confirmed their suspicions that some of their internal

(Continued)

(Continued)

systems did not work as intended and were hampering the potential growth of the business. They decided to write a marketing plan setting clear objectives for growth. This involved taking the following action:

- An overhaul of the company's newsletter. This was their main method of contacting existing and potential customers and they decided to make it more customer-focused by including information such as articles about interview techniques and market briefings that would be useful to their target market. They decided to offer the newsletter by email as well as their existing 'snail mail' option.

- Setting up two new mailing lists for the newsletter – one by email and one by post. These lists consisted of both existing customers and potential customers. Their research had uncovered a number of new companies who were placed on the newsletter mailing lists. They started to receive enquiries straight away from new companies on the list and the feedback they had from customers about the revised content was positive.

- Re-designing the website – they had a website designer produce a much more customer-friendly site and used content from the newsletter and their PR efforts on the site, regularly changing the content to encourage people to visit the site more than just once. They also included a prominent link for the website so that visitors could sign up for their monthly newsletter. This produced a valuable resource in terms of new sales leads.

- Giving a member of staff responsibility for maintenance of the customer database. It was cleaned up with all contact details checked and brought up-to-date, defunct companies deleted from their lists, duplicate entries deleted, more personal information about contacts added plus more detail about the types of companies that were on the list. This resulted in a much more useful database that the consultants had confidence in using and meant that they could market their services much more effectively to existing customers.

- PR activity, including senior management writing articles and getting them published in the trade press. When they conducted further research six months later, they found that this action alone had increased awareness of the company and what they did. They also reproduced these articles on their website and put shortened versions in their monthly newsletter.

The marketing mix after the review was much more customer focused and led to increased business with both existing and new customers as a direct result of the increased customer contact and a more organised approach to marketing. The company kept up the momentum by carrying out these reviews on a regular basis after the initial push and were able to continually improve their market position.

Completing the customer service process – implementation and feedback

As we have said previously, improvement to customer service should not be treated as a one-off process – it must be continually reviewed and subject to continual improvement. However there are two aspects that we need to look at here so that we can be sure that we don't just make ever more complicated plans, work hard and never see any improvements or even know for sure that the plans have worked. First we need to implement all the plans we have made for customer service and then we need to get feedback to be sure that our objectives have been met.

Before you can implement any changes, it is essential that all the staff involved are fully aware not just of what their role is but also of the objectives of the changes. Keeping staff informed is a great motivational tool and is probably the single most important action you can take to ensure the success of the changes. Allocations of responsibility must be clear and also agreed to by the employees involved. In this way, all the members of a team will know what they have to do, why they have to do it and the outcome expected. Any confusion in this area will always adversely affect the plans.

When things are up and running, then you need to be able to take a step back and review exactly what has happened. You need to obtain feedback about your customer service. This can take three forms:

1. Results of KPIs – comparing your KPIs before and after any changes have been implemented will give you hard information as to the results of the changes. Have you met the objectives you set?
2. Feedback from customers – this is 'softer', less tangible information on how customer service is perceived but is nonetheless important in that if your customers are still not satisfied despite the new programme of customer care that you have implemented, then you need to 'go back to the drawing board'. Ultimately, in terms of customer service, the opinions of customers are the most important.
3. Feedback from employees involved – as we have said previously, how members of staff, who are dealing on a

day-to-day basis with customers, feel about the customer service that the organisation is delivering can, in itself, affect customer service. Concerns of these employees must always be taken seriously so it is vital that feedback is obtained – and acted upon.

SUMMARY

In this chapter we have asked the question, 'How can you be sure customers are satisfied?' The point was made that responsibility for good customer service goes throughout the organisation and that it must be given top priority from the very top of the organisation. Most important is fostering the right attitude and this can be done in a number of ways, including producing a mission statement that places customer service firmly in the spotlight and highlights management's support of it. Other things that can be done to improve the general attitude within the organisation towards customer service include getting the right staff (with a pro-customer attitude and experience of dealing with customers), getting training in customer handling for anyone who needs it, implementing visible systems aimed at improving customer service and emphasising the personal touch in all dealings with customers.

It was seen to be important to set clear standards in all the different areas of customer service, including how the initial contact is made, having clear product information available, and having an order procedure, an invoicing system and an after-sales system that, like all other systems in the organisation, have the customer as their focus.

Customer surveys were then discussed – how to plan their use and compose the questions so that a simple, straightforward, customer-friendly but useful questionnaire is produced.

(Continued)

(Continued)

There are many ways of getting information to customers and keeping in touch. The ones suggested here included advertising, customer contact programmes, marketing materials, the media (public relations), responses and follow-ups to complaints, face-to-face or telephone sales and sending information out with invoices, statements etc.

We then completed the process of ensuring the customer is satisfied by discussing implementation and monitoring. Satisfaction is the aim of customer service and must be an ongoing process.

ACTION CHECKLIST

1. Does your organisation have a mission statement? If it does, does it give customer service priority? Could you improve it? If it doesn't, write one that sums up how you feel customer service should be positioned in your organisation.

2. With one aspect of customer service in mind, write three questions for use in a customer survey to investigate that area.

3. Consider how you would use the results to improve customer service.

4. Look at the suggested ways of keeping in touch with your customers. Do you use all of these ways in your organisation? Can you think of other ways?

5. Speak with members of your team to get their opinions on how customer service is dealt with in your organisation.

08

Why does quality matter?

Quality can be defined as a degree or standard of excellence. It is in setting and then achieving that standard that any organisation will ensure that they have the products and services that will sell. 'Quality' in terms of systems and standards in organisations usually refers to the monitoring and measuring of the attainment of the standard that has been set. The quality management system sets out the framework within which the activities of an organisation can be managed, thereby promoting continual improvement.

Quality matters to every organisation because it is only by providing products and services that meet customers' needs and expectations that organisations can gain and retain customers and thereby make a profit or, in the case of non-profit-making organisations, to at least stay in operation. Even a charity, if it does not satisfy its stakeholders, will not last long. Quality standards, when set properly and met, will ensure that products and services are of an acceptable standard – leading to satisfied customers.

Modern approaches to quality have made 'quality control' come to mean that problems with an organisation's products, services and processes are prevented. This is in contrast to the original approach when 'quality control' detected problems by inspection, i.e. when the product was finished.

The place of quality standards in your organisation

A standard is a guideline which, when followed, produces consistency. When an organisation has decided upon the right product, then they need to keep reproducing that product to supply to customers. A lack of control over the quality of a product, i.e. not adhering to the standard that has been set, will result in variations in the product that could well lead to customer dissatisfaction. At this point it is useful to understand that standards must be:

- defined
- observable
- measurable.

So, quality standards must always be aimed at producing a consistent product and satisfying customers. The requirements of the customer should be central to the issue of quality so that organisations do not chase quality for quality's sake but with a purpose – the satisfaction of customers leading to retention of customers. When we aim to improve quality our real aim is to either produce more value for the customer or improve our bottom line. If a quality standard or process cannot be seen to be doing one – or both – of these things, then it is not worth doing.

Apart from increasing customer satisfaction, a further advantage of the use of quality systems in an organisation is that the multiple inspection points laid down in the standards allow problems and mistakes to be detected at all stages of production so that things can be put right before too much time and money has been wasted – an example of where quality can improve the bottom line.

So, it can be seen that implementing a good quality management system can bring many advantages to an organisation. To summarise, these include:

- a recognised quality certification – this can, in effect, provide a reference for your organisation
- quality certification – this can open up new areas of business
- greater consistency in all areas of the business
- better market position – sets you apart from your competitors
- continual improvement system is set up and delivered
- more efficient use of resources
- improved customer service
- reduction in mistakes, saving costs
- induction of new employees is made easier by providing an organisation-wide set of standards.

International standards

To get the full range of benefits from implementing a quality management system it is necessary to gain accreditation to a recognised standard. The ISO 9001:2000 standard is the most widely recognised international standard and over 60,000 UK companies have achieved this certification. This standard demands commitment to quality from senior management, ensures customer satisfaction by measuring a wide range of standards, is used throughout a business to improve all the different aspects of service delivery and production, and also provides a check on matters such as the working environment, staffing levels and use of resources.

Implementing a quality management system and gaining ISO 9001:2000 accreditation has, as we have already seen, many advantages for an organisation but it can take up a lot of time – especially in the initial stages – and can cost a substantial sum of money to implement, especially if, like most companies, you have to engage the services of a quality consultant to assist with implementation.

Most businesses who have implemented a quality management system choose to have it certified by an accredited body. This may be because their customers or suppliers require them to be certified or simply to improve their reputation and enable them to gain more business in the UK and abroad. Certification involves assessment by an accredited body such as those that are members of the United Kingdom Accreditation Service. You will need to prepare for this assessment by making sure that all the documentation in your quality management system is in order. If you are unable to present the correct documentation for assessment or if there are parts of your system that are deemed by the representative of the certification body not to be up to standard, then he or she will discuss corrective action with you and may arrange a time for another assessment.

Even after you have received certification, the accredited body will still keep an eye on your systems to keep your accreditation valid. This will take the form of twice-yearly visits. This can make a quality system an expensive and time-consuming undertaking for any organisation, but it is generally felt to be a worthwhile investment as the returns in terms of a more efficient and effective business are obvious.

To go a step further than accreditation to ISO 9001:2000, many companies use the ISO 9004:2000 standard as guidance on continual improvement. This is a set of recommendations (so accreditation to this particular standard cannot be applied for) that can be used as a framework for improving a business. It consists of eight principles of quality management, which are summarised here:

1. Senior management should show strong leadership.
2. All staff should be involved in the success of the business.
3. There must be a focus on customers in the business.
4. All business activities should be identified as part of a process.

5. Systems should be in place to ensure that all business processes are managed together.
6. All decision makers should be fully informed.
7. The organisation should have mutually dependent relationships with suppliers.
8. Continual improvement should be a prime business objective.

By following these quality management principles not only will a more profitable business result, but it will also ensure that employees, suppliers and everyone involved will benefit.

Apart from the internationally recognised quality systems mentioned here, there are also sector-specific quality standards that may apply to your organisation and these should usually be given priority over the generic ones.

Legal and regulatory requirements

One of the responsibilities of a quality management system is to ensure that all business processes comply with all regulations. The quality requirements that your organisation has to meet legally will depend upon the industry or sector that you are in. Many sectors are highly regulated and there will be legal requirements for the organisation to carry out certain functions to a particular quality standard, for example:

- dealing with hazardous chemicals
- the transport industry
- the care of children.

Putting quality systems in place

There is a sequence of events that will ensure success in putting a quality system in place in any organisation:

1. Commitment – from the top and throughout the organisation. Without that commitment it will be almost impossible to install any effective quality management system as it takes hard work and a clear vision of what the organisation is trying to achieve.
2. Knowing customers' needs and expectations – if you don't know what your customers want then you must put measures in place that will give you this information (see also Chapter 3).
3. Designing products and services that meet your customers' needs and expectations.
4. Deciding on standards to be met – these will extend not just to the products but to the support personnel's dealings with customers, and to internal customers and suppliers too.
5. Setting up a management system to manage quality, ensuring that the right products and services are faithfully repeated with each delivery. Any system for quality management must ensure that each and every employee takes personal responsibility for achieving the standards that have been set and for reporting errors along the way. This can often need a culture change and is one of the more difficult aspects of quality management.
6. Making sure that no products or services are supplied to customers that do not meet the quality standards that have been set. Where errors or a shortfall in quality are detected, it is vital that the error is reported and

corrected and then, as soon as possible, the causes should be investigated and remedial action put in place.

7. Commitment to continual improvement – see the section later in this chapter. The main thing is that a system for continual improvement is in place and results in significant benefits for the organisation at a reasonable cost.

There are several generic quality management systems in current use in the UK. These include ISO 9001:2000 (discussed earlier), TQM (Total Quality Management), Lean Manufacturing and Investors in People. Following any of these systems (or outsourcing the area of quality management) will result in a workable system being set up. However, unless the implementation is supported and worked at by all stakeholders there will be problems and quality is unlikely to improve appreciably.

Case study

A small chain of nurseries and playgroups decided to implement a quality management system and found that, although the work took some time and they initially met resistance from staff, it had a positive effect on the business.

As the company was dealing with children they felt that trust and their reputation were very important to the business and that ISO 9001:2000 certification would be a benefit to them.

They started by conducting a review of their current systems and appointed a senior manager as Quality Manager. They also engaged a local quality consultant who identified the areas in need of improvement in order to gain accreditation and improve the business. These areas included their purchasing system, record keeping and methods of obtaining customer feedback.

(Continued)

(Continued)

After a few months the new processes had been documented in a quality manual to which everyone could refer and the new systems had been implemented.

They found that communicating the objectives of the new emphasis on quality and details about operating the new systems to their staff was crucial to the success of the project. They did this by holding an initial presentation, individual meetings with staff and letters to each of them setting out the aims and how each member of staff could help to achieve them. Some staff were particularly resistant to the changes, but the many-pronged approach to communication won them over.

As part of the new systems, targets were set that would help them to achieve and monitor the improvement. These included a target for the reduction of costs of goods purchased and the number of customer feedback forms that should be obtained and properly logged. As a result, after a few months of the new systems having been put in place, costs were down by 4 per cent and nearly 25 per cent more customer feedback forms were obtained. The emphasis on the feedback forms resulted in a concentration on resolving issues rather than putting them to one side as they had done in the past.

Regular audits, that the organisation has to complete to retain their ISO 9001:2000 accreditation, have meant that they continually monitor their performance against the standards that have been set.

The nursery group are now looking at further expansion and they credit the implementation of the quality system with being the catalyst for the change and improvement that they so badly needed.

Preparing for a quality audit

A quality audit will prove an organisation's success – or otherwise – in meeting the standards that have been set. It checks that the quality system is operating as intended. Quality audits can be internal or external. If the audit you are preparing for is external, then it is likely that you will have received some guidance on preparation from the auditing body, but it should go without saying that you should conduct a check of your quality systems so that you are confident everything is in place. If, on the other hand, you are taking part in an internal audit you will not only have to ensure that your quality systems are in place and up to date but also to make sure that you have had the necessary training in auditing procedures.

Depending on the scope of the audit to be carried out it can be useful to inform members of staff that they will have to supply samples for examination. These may be samples of products for analysis, examples of how customers have been dealt with, departmental records for checking and so on. This sort of preparation is not meant to provide an opportunity to falsify any records or to affect the overall result of the audit, but is aimed at smoothing the path of what can be a long, complicated procedure that would be made problematic by someone not being available to lay their hands on a document, for example.

Internal audits are an essential part of any formal quality management system and must be carried out at regular intervals. As they should usually be carried out by someone who is not involved in the day-to-day running of a department, it is likely that if you are asked to take part in an internal quality audit, you will be auditing an area with which you are not particularly familiar. This can be an interesting experience and will serve to broaden your knowledge of your organisation.

Getting involved in quality audits

Quality audits should be viewed as an opportunity to prove that everything is running as it should be. If errors are thrown up during the audit then this is the ideal chance to learn from mistakes.

Good preparation, including ensuring that all relevant documentation is up to date and readily available, will result in a successful outcome. Regular audits produce three main benefits:

1. The organisation's ability to reach its objectives is enhanced. This includes increasing sales, selling products into new markets and developing new products. Following an audit, information is produced that will increase an organisation's effectiveness and reduce the risk of failure.
2. The risk of liability is reduced. If products that are not up to standard are produced and sent out to customers rather than being stopped by the quality system, then claims against the organisation could ensue. This also applies to services, as quality systems (including audits) can ensure that risks are not taken with, for example, customers' information or that customers are not put in any danger by a service supplied by the organisation.
3. The company is made more efficient – the same goods (or services) are produced at lower cost as a result of the reduction in wasted resources.

These three advantages mean that it is well worth cooperating with audit requirements as there is a clear business case to show that these benefits will contribute to the organisation's effectiveness and, where appropriate, its profitability.

Thorough preparation is essential to get the most benefit for your organisation from a quality audit. Before the audit begins you should find out:

- the exact scope of the audit
- the responsibilities of the department to be audited
- what quality procedures apply in the department
- what has happened in previous audits.

Following the audit, any non-conformances that have been uncovered during the audit must be dealt with by the agreed dates. Any possible improvements to processes must be identified and work started on putting them into place. The actions to be taken following an audit must be agreed with the auditor.

Continual improvement

Continual improvement is closely allied to quality standards and systems. It is about the whole organisation and requires commitment from the top right the way through the organisation in the same way that quality standards do. It is not sufficient to have a quality policy statement signed by the Managing Director or to have a large quality department working on ever-more complicated systems. Everyone in the organisation must buy in to the idea that things can be done better and that that will ensure the success and longevity of the organisation for the good of everyone, from bosses and employees to shareholders, customers and suppliers. Continual improvement, put simply, means getting better all the time. Everything can be a target for continual improvement – relationships with customers, suppliers and employees, business strategies and results. It is about changing things so that the effectiveness of an organisation is increased so that it is better able to fulfil objectives and get results.

Continual improvement requires a real change in culture in most organisations and the setting-up of a quality management system can help with this. There may be several elements that stop improvement from taking place:

- resistance to change
- fear of reporting problems or errors
- lack of desire to share ideas
- inertia
- hanging on to the status quo – the 'if it isn't broke, don't fix it' mentality.

There are ten steps that will help to attain continual improvement:

1. Find out where you are now – this is your baseline. It could be how quickly your call centre operatives answer the phone, the amount of spoiled goods that are produced on a production line or maybe the employee retention rate – whatever you want to improve.
2. Decide whether you need to improve.
3. Define your objective and, at this point, get commitment to the improvement from everyone involved.
4. Put systems in place to analyse what you are currently doing and how.
5. Get the results of the analysis and decide why your current performance is as it is.
6. Decide on the improvement strategy that will deliver the objective.
7. Produce detailed plans as to how, by whom and when the necessary work will be carried out.
8. Deal with any resistance. Whenever there is change there will be resistance and this can derail any improvement plans so it is essential to identify and deal with it at an early stage.
9. Implement the changes.

10. Make sure that you have systems in place to check on the new processes and to monitor the improvements achieved.

Finally, an important part of any continual improvement policy in any organisation is that of reward. Anyone who has initiated an improvement, however small, must be recognised. This will not only encourage the individual involved to look for further improvements but will also help to persuade other employees to suggest improvements. The reward does not have to be financial – it could be something as simple as being made 'employee of the month' with their photo on a special 'improvements' notice board, a mention in the company magazine or a small prize. It is important that the style of any recognition and accompanying campaign to get suggestions for improvements fits in with the organisation's style. A flashy, celebrity-style campaign would not go well within a staid office environment, for example, and may lead to criticism of the campaign rather than the desired result of motivating staff.

The implementation of a quality management system will be invaluable in attaining a culture of continuous improvement as quality standards and continual improvement go hand in hand.

SUMMARY

In answering the question, 'Why does quality matter?', we first had to define quality. It is a standard which, when met, produces consistency. It is a useful tool in ensuring and increasing customer satisfaction. We then looked at what it takes to gain accreditation of a quality management system to a recognised standard such as ISO 9001:2000.

A quality management system can help an organisation to comply with legal and regulatory requirements such as those associated with hazardous chemicals, transport and childcare.

(Continued)

(Continued)

Next, we examined the sequence of actions that should be followed to develop a quality management system – commitment from the top, knowledge of customer needs, setting and meeting standards and finally a commitment to continual improvement.

Guidance was given for preparing and taking part in quality audits and the advantages they bring such as increasing effectiveness and efficiency and reducing the risk of liability were outlined.

We then went through the ten steps that will help to ensure continual improvement starting with deciding where you are now and where you want to be, followed by analysis of current systems, planning how to improve, dealing with resistance and changing systems as necessary. We also discussed offering rewards as part of the improvement culture.

ACTION CHECKLIST

1. Check out the quality management system in your own organisation and assess how it helps to ensure customer satisfaction. If your organisation does not have a quality management system, assess how implementing one could improve customer service.
2. Find evidence of the commitment – or lack of it – that your senior management has to quality in your organisation.
3. Find out who conducts audits in your organisation.
4. Plan a small change that could improve customer service in your organisation.
5. Consider the advantages and disadvantages of offering rewards for meeting improvement targets.

09

Have you got the right product or service?

This is a question that every entrepreneur and senior manager should ask on a regular basis. Although you may have hit on just the right thing for your market in the initial stages of your organisation's development, markets change. Your products or services must therefore change in accordance with what the market demands. You should also consider that although your product may still be in demand, the method of delivery may change. For example, supermarkets still sell a lot of the food products that they originally offered many years ago, but today there is a desire from a significant proportion of customers to be able to buy the products online and have them delivered, as well as going to the supermarket themselves and buying them off the shelves. Also, it should be noted that all products have a lifecycle and it is important to know just where your product or service is in its lifecycle. Continual product development and innovation will ensure that your organisation grows and maintains profitability. A good marketing strategy will always include thorough examinations of current and future product offers, strengths and weaknesses of the organisation, the competition and the market.

First, you need to know everything about your product and its place in the market.

Knowing your product

It is important that you know your product because if you don't fully understand all about what you are offering, then you will not be able to sell your products or services effectively. With the right information about your product and about your customers' requirements you can persuade other organisations that they need to buy from you.

One way to ensure that you know your products is to consider each individual product's unique selling point (USP). A USP is what makes your product or service different. It is what makes it stand out from the competition. Standing out from the competition is vital to your organisation's success, so to beat your competitors you will need to show that you are either better at providing the goods or services or that you are cheaper. Knowing a product's USP is how you will be able to show this differentiation. This USP may be that a DVD player is easier to use than equivalent models offered by the competition, for example, or that it has been designed to solve a particular problem.

Identifying a product's USP will show you the key aspects of your product and you will therefore understand why your customers buy your products. This will give greater focus to your advertising and sales activities, making them more effective. So, how should you go about finding a USP? First you should list all the features of the product you are examining, then convert all these features into benefits.

Knowing the benefits of your products or services is important because customers buy benefits rather than features. In the example above, you may consider 'ease of use' to be very important, but your customer is likely to think that cutting down on training costs is more important.

INSTANT TIP

'Features' describe what your product or service does. These might include quality, reliability, service, delivery, price and technical aspects. 'Benefits' show what the customer can get from it. A useful way of converting a feature into a benefit is to use the words 'which means that' after each feature. For example, if a feature of a machine is that it is easy to use, then the benefit may be that it does not require the machine's operators to be highly trained, saving on training costs (i.e. one of the machine's feature is its ease of use 'which means that' it does not require the machine's operators to be highly trained, saving on training costs).

It should be noted here that although we have been concentrating so far on discovering the USPs of our products and services, an organisation will also have a unique selling point. It might be that you are cheaper than your competitors or that your quality is known to be higher. It can also change over the life of your business because the goals may change or you may have to change in response to developments in the market in which you operate.

USPs give your customers a reason to buy so, whatever you decide are your USPs for your business or for your products, they must match your customers' requirements.

Having decided what a product's USP is, and also maybe what your organisation's USP is, you must then ensure that you use this information to best effect in all your sales and marketing efforts.

Another aspect of knowing your products and services are the technical specifications and the various regulatory requirements applicable to your product. Depending on the type of products and services you supply, this could include:

- safety regulations
- food safety
- data protection requirements
- import requirements
- EU regulations
- product registration
- restrictions on organic goods production
- pharmaceutical regulations
- financial products regulation
- Sale of Goods Act
- export and import restrictions.

This list is not exhaustive but gives you examples of the breadth of information you may need about your products and services. A thorough knowledge of the technical aspects of your products is also essential.

How do your customers perceive your product?

Now that you have thoroughly investigated your product and know its unique selling point, what it can do, how it is made, what regulations it must comply with and what it offers to your customers in terms of benefits, you will need to turn your attention to what your customers think of it. They will not see your products in the same way that you do and sometimes it can be difficult, being so close to something, to see any alternative view. Yet again, you will need to ask your customers their opinions. Ask them what they think your organisation's USP is or the USP for a particular product that they buy. Their answer may be different to what you have decided. The customers' views are, of course, more important. After all, as we said, a USP gives a customer a reason to buy, so what they think should be taken seriously.

Asking your existing customers about their perception of your products and services can be a very useful exercise and you have choices to make about how you carry this out. The first, and most obvious, decision is who will carry out the survey – will you do it yourself or engage the services of a professional market research organisation?

If you decide to carry out the research in-house then you will need to be clear about what resources – in terms of staff time and financial budget – you are prepared, or able, to make available for it. It may seem that doing it yourself is a cheaper option but you should take into account what the staff you allocate to the task of finding out what your customers think would be doing if they weren't occupied with the survey. If you can see that you will lose sales or that your customer service will suffer then it may be a false economy. However, professional research can be expensive so if you decide to go it alone here are a few points to remember when compiling a survey (also look back at Chapter 7 for more detail on how to conduct your own survey):

- Decide who you will ask – you may decide to pick out larger customers or ones who have been with you for some time. It is important that you ask sufficient numbers of customers to get a representative view but not so many that the results are unmanageable.
- Make sure your customer database is up to date and as correct as you can make it.
- Ask the right person – you should be able to direct the survey to the right person in the organisation by consulting your customer database.
- Decide what you will ask – keep the questions simple and straightforward but make sure that you concentrate on finding out your customers' perception of your products or services.

- Keep it impartial – try not to elicit the answers that you want to see. Unless you can obtain your customers' honest opinions and views then the survey will have been a waste of time and money.
- Set up systems for the recording, monitoring and analysing of the returned surveys.
- Use the results – unless the surveys confirm exactly what you thought you would find (in which case, are you sure you asked the right questions and that you weren't biased?) then you will need to make changes to your products and services. This could just be 'fine tuning' what you are offering to make sure that you are giving your customers what they want, or it could mean a major shift in the focus of your entire business. The important thing is to act on what you find out.

One of the best ways of getting comprehensive and relatively unbiased information about your customers' perceptions of your products is to commission a report from an independent market research organisation. In considering whether or not to engage a company who specialises in conducting market research, you should take into account the following:

- How much time and money you could devote to doing the job internally. Compare this with the likely cost of outsourcing the work.
- Your customers may find a professional researcher's approach more acceptable. If you ask them a lot of questions they may view the survey as a way of selling them something and be very suspicious of it. In contrast, a research agency's approach will be neutral and will not arouse your customer's suspicions. This may, of course, result in the agency obtaining better, more truthful responses.

- A professional researcher will know what questions to ask and will have experience in designing and conducting surveys, holding focus groups and then dealing with the results. Again, this should mean you get a truer picture.
- Using a professional agency will ensure that the survey is impartial.

Choosing a research agency requires some work on your part. Recommendation is usually the best way of finding someone reliable but will still require you to check out their credentials and make sure that their approach is appropriate to your purpose. If you don't have any recommendations then you will need to find a reputable agency or freelance researcher yourself. Your local Chamber of Commerce may be able to help or, failing that, many freelance researchers and market research agencies have a web presence. It is also worth consulting BusinessLink and LinkedIn. In any event, always check:

- that the agency or researcher has relevant experience
- references – get the names and addresses of previous customers of the agency and check them out; ask them just what work the agency carried out for them and how satisfied they were
- the rates – be clear about what you would be getting for your money
- that you feel comfortable with the people you would be working with
- that they have the relevant licences and permissions – this is especially important if they will be carrying out street interviews for you.

After selecting the right researcher for your organisation, you must brief the research company thoroughly. You must be clear about what you are trying to achieve and that the researcher thoroughly understands the business objectives that are driving the project.

They may then telephone or write to your customers to elicit this information. Other methods could include street interviews, focus groups and sampling. They will then analyse the information and usually make recommendations as to how the results of their survey can best be used to improve your product marketing and perhaps how you can develop your products to increase sales and/or profitability.

It is important that as part of this process you understand why your customers see your products as they do. What do your advertising and other marketing efforts tell them? Are you using the benefits of your products in your marketing or simply highlighting their features? Does your product literature portray the image that you intended? Try to look at every piece of information that goes out of your company with a dispassionate eye to discover what has influenced your customers' views. It is only when you understand what their perceptions are and what you may have done to make them form these views that you will be able to make sure that your products meet the needs of the market and that you are describing them and selling them to best effect.

Competitiveness

The world has become increasingly competitive so that a customer is faced with many choices of supplier no matter what they are intending to purchase. It is important to note that this does not just apply to commercial transactions but also applies to non-profit-making organisations – we all have a choice, for example, about which charity we support with our donations or voluntary work. The pace of life has speeded up in recent years and living standards have increased so that getting a prompt reply from a company, or an immediate delivery rather than waiting a week or two as may have been the case in the past has gained in importance. In more competitive markets, customers are becoming increasingly knowledgeable about what is available so they have become more selective and will need a reason to support one organisation over another. Most businesses operate in a sophisticated environment so that buyers are inundated with information – clever advertising, internet comparison sites, the organisations' own websites, surveys, consumer groups' reports and so on. This all means that competitors will be putting more and more effort and resources into becoming the buyers' first choice. One of the ways to do this is by improving customer care, including making sure that you are offering the right product at the right price.

Knowing your competition

Knowing exactly who your competitors are and what they are doing is vitally important to any organisation. If you are not familiar with all aspects of your competition and what they are offering to your customers and potential customers, then your knowledge of your business is incomplete. You will not be able to formulate comprehensive plans to maximise your sales and your profits may suffer. Without this vital knowledge you will not know what you are doing well and what you are doing badly by comparison and will therefore not be able to make improvements to your performance. You will also be missing out on a valuable source of ideas.

It is important to understand that every organisation has competitors. It may be the straightforward, market-driven competition that we are all familiar with – such as the supermarkets that compete for our money every day of the week – or it may be more subtle like the different charities that try to get us to donate money or time. They are all competing in one way or another. Wherever there are customers, or something to be gained, there will be competition for the resources. There is competition in internal markets as well as external, but in this section we will be concentrating on external competitors. In this case, competitors can be defined as organisations providing something that could be seen as an alternative to what your organisation provides. So, for example, if you produce books your competitors will not only be other book publishers but also website content producers and e-books available for download on the internet or, in some cases, magazines and newspapers. You could also consider organisations offering alternative forms of entertainment as competitors, as people going out more could mean that you sell fewer books. Remember, we are competing for resources.

The first step in making sure that you win the battle for resources is to identify who your competition is. If you have been in a business for some time you will probably already be aware of most of your competition, but research will produce more detailed information and may throw up some surprising results. So, where can you get information about who your competitors are? Try the following sources:

- **Local and national newspapers** – see who is advertising, who is looking for new staff, who has announced a new product launch, who is building a new factory or who is announcing redundancies.
- **The internet** – try searching for similar products to yours and see which companies come up first in your searches. This is a sign that they are putting resources into internet marketing.
- **Chambers of Commerce and local business organisations** – they will have extensive information about local businesses and any organisations of which your business is a member will usually let you search their library of information or may give advice about the state of the market in your area compiled from the extensive research they carry out.
- **Ask your customers** – who else do they buy from, who is making special offers to them, are they considering new products?

- **Ask your suppliers** – do they supply your competitors too? They may tell you about new customers in the market, increased or decreased sales to some of your competitors and what products are going well, for instance.
- **Exhibitions and conferences**– who is attending, who is exhibiting, who is speaking at conferences?
- **Planning applications** – you can see if local competitors are extending their premises or if new companies who may be competition for you are coming into the area.
- **Marketing materials** – any that you receive in the course of business or at home may point you to areas of competition.

All of these areas of research will not only give you information about your competitors but should also give you ideas about how you can improve your own business's performance and how you can publicise your organisation's goods or services.

So, having found out exactly who is in competition with you, your next task is to get some detail about your competitors' businesses such as:

Products

What do they provide? Are their products and services similar to yours? Find out, if you can, how much they are currently selling of each type of product. How do your products or services compare? Look in detail at all aspects of what your organisation offers and your competitors' products. Done properly this will give you lots of information. You should examine the products in terms of their technical aspects as well as their more aesthetic characteristics and also check out packaging and how the advertising and marketing is put together for both ranges.

Prices

How do their prices compare with yours? Get hold of price lists by requesting them online or by phone. You may need to get a friend to do this for you if you feel they would not give you this information. If their prices are lower, consider how they keep prices low and, if they are higher, how much does this affect their sales levels? Do you need to review your own pricing structure in light of this information?

Customers

Who are their customers? Do you have customers in common? Do they have a constantly changing customer base or have they got a substantial proportion of long-standing customers? Decide where there are overlaps and also where your competitors have the edge. You can then make plans, if applicable, to target these customers with your own campaign using the information about your products and theirs that you have discovered.

Media activity

Monitor local and national press, radio and television and the trade press as appropriate to see how much space they get and what they are publicising. If you keep an eye on the appropriate media channels you will get a great deal of information about what your competitors are up to, new developments and so on.

Marketing materials

It is often possible to request these from websites. Check them out to find out if they are professional-looking and what approach they are taking. Their product literature may give technical specifications which could prove useful in comparing their product offer with yours. You should pay particular attention to any recently launched products as these will indicate where the company plans to go with their product range and may be a reason for you to review the product range offered by your organisation.

Websites

Look at their websites. Do they do a good job of selling to customers? Are they an easy-to-use source of information that their customers and prospective customers will go back to time after time? What image of the business do they present? Is it traditional or modern? Look for lots of information about the organisation often placed on websites that might be difficult to find elsewhere, such as company history, board member details, staff profiles and so on. You should also make a comparison with your own website and look for ways that you could improve your own approach.

The market

How are your competitors viewed in the market? This could be termed their image and you should already be familiar with how your organisation is viewed so a comparison will be useful. You can then change what you do in terms of PR and advertising to present a more positive image for your own organisation.

Sales methods

How do they sell to their customers? Find out what size and type of sales force they have, whether they use agents, how much they depend on telesales, how much of their business, if any, comes from online sales and how much from mail order. Have they changed any of these sales channels in recent times? This can give you a pointer to how their business is changing and reacting to current pressures. For example, if they already have substantial online sales then this is likely to increase in importance in the next few years but if they do not currently sell anything via their website then, if this is an appropriate method of selling for their particular products, that may be an area that they are missing out on. How do your competitors get their products to the market? Consider whether they – and you – use a third party (such as retail outlets or agents) to sell their goods and, if so, are their arrangements better or worse than yours?

Customer service

What is the standard and reputation of their customer service? Your own customers will often be able to help you with this sort of information and will often be pleased to discuss this with you if you present your enquiry in terms of improving your own service. If they buy from your competitors as well as your organisation they will obviously have experience of the service but if they don't buy from them then the standard of service may well be one of the reasons. You need to find out where your competitors are stronger than you and then improve your performance in those areas. Do they have a customer loyalty programme, a customer help line and so on?

People

How many people do your competitors employ? Compare that with the financial size or sales of their company to see what their staffing ratios are. Are they higher or lower than yours? Do you need more staff to match their level of service or could you manage with less? Although changes of this type are not ones to be undertaken lightly, it is a point to consider during and after your research.

Logistics

How do your competitors deliver their goods and services to customers? Which transport companies do they use? Find out if their deliveries are prompt and reliable.

Suppliers

Who are their major suppliers? In many cases, their suppliers will also supply your organisation but if not, it can be useful to investigate the suppliers they are using. Are they cheaper than your regular suppliers? Do they supply a superior quality of product?

Brand

How important is their brand? Have they consistently promoted their brand and invested in it? Is it well known – maybe in your area, in your industry or internationally?

Finances

Are they profitable? You can find out this and lots of other financial details by accessing their accounts at Companies House. This will give you a picture of their activities from a financial viewpoint and you can compare how they are doing with your own position, taking into account the relative size of the two companies. If it is a public company there will be an annual report for you to examine.

Community

What is their attitude to the community? If you are looking at a local competitor, note how much involvement with the area they have. Some companies gain valuable coverage in the local press as a result of their charity support or taking part in community projects such as sponsorship of youth clubs. This not only raises an organisation's profile in the local area but also affects people's attitudes to the company, which can prove useful in gaining support – or at least a lack of opposition – if planning permission is required for new industrial or commercial buildings or in encouraging local people to apply for jobs with the company, making recruitment easier.

Strengths and weaknesses

What are their strengths, opportunities and weaknesses? You will probably find it useful to do a SWOT analysis of your main competitors (more about how to do this later in this chapter) as this may highlight areas that you will need to change or take advantage of. What are their plans for the future?

Future plans

Are they developing new products? Are they expanding or changing direction?

INSTANT TIP

More detailed information could be obtained via a professional market research agency.

As you can see, the information you can look into about your competitors is almost endless, but the more you know about them, the more you will be able to compete. Don't be afraid of making comparisons between your own organisation and others. You will inevitably pick up information about business approaches that will improve your own business. If you analyse the information you have found, you will be able to pick out the strengths and weaknesses of your competitors and then use the information to your own advantage.

If there are things that your competitors are doing better than you then you will need to improve your own organisation's performance in that area. Don't just copy what your competitors do, use their example as the basis of a real change in your own organisation so that you also improve on what they are doing.

When you're having a close look at your competitors you will need to keep in mind a lot of information about your own organisation and the products or services you offer so that you can make the comparisons with your competitors and see where you will be able to improve your performance.

Where you find that your organisation's performance is superior then make sure that you capitalise on that. If, for example, you find that their prices are generally higher than yours, you could consider letting your customers know what a bargain they're getting.

Finally, remember that while you are assessing your competitors they may well be checking you out. It is important that you do not become complacent, as any areas where you can be seen to be better than your customers could easily be just the area that they have spotted and are in the process of improving. Things change all the time in business so research and subsequent improvement should be ongoing.

INSTANT TIP

Be wary of information supplied to you. A lot of the information you get about your competitors will be given to you by your customers and suppliers who will have their own interests to look after. Price information, for example, may not be reliable if what your customer wants is for you to reduce your prices.

If you do not fully understand how your customers differentiate between you and your competitors then it will be impossible to make meaningful decisions about any possible improvements you can make to your products and to your marketing strategy. As you examine each aspect of your products and those of your competitors you should note what you do better and also what your competitors do better. You will be able to see what to keep and what to change and how you can borrow ideas from your competitors that will help you improve.

Following on from this comparison of your products or services and those offered by your competitors, you should summarise what you have found out about the market in which you operate by preparing a list of your organisation's strengths and weaknesses.

An ideal way to do this is to do a SWOT analysis – Strengths, Weaknesses, Opportunities and Threats.

For example, your Strengths could include:

- a product that is well established in the market
- your organisation's reputation
- good customer service

Weaknesses could include:

- a weak sales force
- a poor reputation
- manufacturing processes that need updating

Opportunities could include:

- developing a new stream of business via the internet
- a competitor in difficulties
- investment in new plant

Threats could include:

- reducing demand for your product
- new competitors in the market
- competitors using other technologies such as the internet to reach their customers

Each element of this SWOT analysis should inform your marketing strategy. Having gathered all the details together and decided how important each competitor is to your organisation, you will be able to start work on revising your marketing strategy.

Case study

An IT contracting business decided to use analysis of competitors to help to drive improvements in the business. They started by drawing up a list of their main competitors. They quickly realised that it would be impossible to analyse all the firms working in IT in their area so they limited it to companies who provided very similar services and were of a certain size or above, ruling out 'one man bands'. They then decided what they wanted to know about these competitors including:

- pricing policy
- impressions of customer service
- qualifications held by staff
- training policy.

They felt that their company was relatively strong in these areas but they needed to be sure and also to see what they could learn from their competitors. The actions they took to find information about these competitors included:

- Contacting all the companies on the list by telephone. They requested marketing materials and recorded how long they took to arrive. They also monitored the response times to the phone calls to check efficiency and customer service in that area.
- Examining their competitors' literature for quality, content and marketing approach.
- Checking out their competitors' websites.
- Reviewing trade journals to see what presence – in terms of both advertising and articles – their competition had.
- Looking for recruitment advertising to see what qualifications they were asking of applicants, salary levels and so on.

- Speaking to as many of their customers and suppliers as possible about the competition in the market.

Following this extensive research they compiled a report that assessed the effectiveness and position of each of their key competitors. They found that, as they had suspected, many of their competitors were slow to answer telephone enquiries and had websites that were not user-friendly. Their next step was to use the results of their research to improve their own performance. In particular, they checked their own telephone response times and, although they compared favourably, put in place targets to ensure a quick answer in the majority of cases as they realised that the phones left ringing by their competitors were annoying to both potential and existing customers. They also reformulated their human resources policy to incorporate some of the terms and conditions that they had found were on offer in their market.

With the success in improving performance and the boost that being compared favourably gave to both staff and management they decided to carry out the exercise on a regular basis and used the results to drive continual performance improvement.

Developing a marketing strategy

A marketing strategy is vital to any business to ensure that the approach to the products or services to be offered, to the markets to be served, and to attaining sales and customer satisfaction, is cohesive and effective. It should also be capable of changing over time to allow for market changes.

Any marketing strategy should have a number of aims:

- making the most of the existing product range and resources available by matching them to the needs of the different groups of customers
- expanding sales through increasing market share
- expanding the product range
- finding new markets
- setting out the ways in which the product or service will be marketed
- retaining existing customers – research has shown that it can be more expensive to find a new customer than to retain an old one so, when you are building a marketing strategy in an effort to maximise profits, don't forget to include your existing customer base.

INSTANT TIP

Before you analyse your customer database make sure that it is correct and up to date. This can be time consuming but is worth doing as it can reveal errors and entries that should be removed from the database that would result in a waste of your marketing efforts.

The main purposes of a marketing strategy are to identify your market (hopefully all the work you've done in comparing your product offer with that of your competitors will help here) and then to get the word out to your existing and prospective customers in the most effective way possible.

While your data and analysis are vital to your marketing strategy, you will also need to be aware of your organisation's corporate objectives so that you can be sure that your marketing plan is in line with them. So, take your SWOT analysis, your data on your competitors and about your product, plus any external research you may have access to, and start to lay out a cohesive and comprehensive marketing plan. This will have several stages:

1. Set your marketing objectives. This will detail what you want to achieve.
2. Make a plan for achieving each element of your marketing objectives – this will include details of the products you intend to offer, the prices you charge for your products and services, how you intend to promote your products and the market(s) in which you intend to operate.
3. Decide who will do what – and how.
4. Define the resources needed to achieve your objectives.
5. Get the plan on paper. Keep this brief by confining it to the essential information – see later in this section.
6. Get your message out. If your objectives and the plan to achieve them are not properly communicated to everyone who has a part to play in the success, then the plan will undoubtedly fail.
7. As always, the plan should be monitored to evaluate its success. Don't be afraid to change what isn't working.
8. Review the plan regularly. As circumstances and markets change you will need to keep your marketing plan up to date.

It can be helpful to have some questions in mind when formulating a marketing strategy following the steps above. Try asking yourself:

- What do we want to achieve?
- Which customers are most profitable? Knowing where the most profitable of your sales come from means that you know where to concentrate most of your efforts.
- What are customers looking for? Don't make assumptions – do your research.

- Are our products priced correctly?
- What's the best way of communicating with customers?
- How is our customer service? Does it need improvement? (See also Chapters 5, 6 and 7.)
- Have we got the right products? (See the next section for more on this.)
- Are our existing customers also buying something else from others and could I also offer them this?
- Do we need to do more advertising, attend more trade fairs, do better PR or more direct marketing?
- How will we tell if the plan is effective? (See later in this chapter for more information on monitoring results.)

When writing up your marketing plan make sure it is easy to follow, brief and structured. The elements to include are:

- a brief introduction and overview
- the marketing objectives – relate these to the corporate objectives and priorities
- a summary of the strategy including costs and timescales together with the benefits to the organisation that are anticipated
- the plan – complete with details of who will do what and when
- the budget
- plans for monitoring the success of the plan
- a conclusion.

Your aim is to come up with a marketing plan that takes into account all the important aspects of your marketing strategy – your organisation's aims, the actions you need to take to achieve them, when you will take each of the necessary actions, what resources you will use and how you will sell your products or services. It should include details about your customers and their requirements and should focus on the area of the market where you can be most successful.

Are you offering a similar product to your competitors?

In many market sectors there will be great similarity in the products on offer and it can seem difficult to ascertain how a customer will make their choice as to which company to buy from. The answer is differentiation in areas other than the product. One such area is customer care. If an organisation has built up a reputation for effective customer service and support this can enable a buyer to make a choice between otherwise similar offerings.

Customers are becoming more willing to support a company that offers good customer service as they know that the problems caused by poor service – returning goods, having to request replacements products, taking time to complain, waiting for information, being let down on delivery dates – are a significant cost to their business. All businesses will be – or certainly should be – continually searching for ways to reduce their costs so finding reliable suppliers who will not cause them problems has become a priority for most organisations. Customers will certainly not continue to support an organisation that offers a similar product to other companies but that is backed up by poor customer service. Poor customer service in this case results in lost business.

Price pressure

Good customer service can even reduce price pressure, which can be more of an issue during an economic downturn. While most organisations will say that buying a product at the lowest possible price is their aim, they will not, as we have already said, usually stay with a supplier who offers poor customer service – no matter how cheap the product or service. So, improving customer service – and letting your customers and potential customers know that this is a priority for you – is one way of overcoming price pressure and increasing profit. A reputation for excellent customer service can enable an organisation to command a premium price for their products and to resist pressure to reduce prices even in a very competitive market.

However, standards of customer service aside, an organisation's prices should be regularly reviewed. This will ensure that the business remains profitable and will also take into account developments in the market or changes that your competitors may make. If you find that you need to change your prices – for example, you may be facing increased price pressure in the market so want to try to reduce your prices or have had to accept increases in costs that mean your current prices no longer allow you to make a profit – then it must be done very carefully. Whether raising or lowering prices, you must be aware of the effect that the change will have on the volume of sales and also the effect on profit margins.

If you need to lower your prices, you must first check the effect on your profitability. If you can't make a profit at the prices you set then you won't be in business for long. So, the decision to lower prices needs a lot of thought. Consider what effect the lower prices may have on your company's image – many buyers will equate low prices with poor quality. Making the decision to buy is rarely simply a matter of price. Could you do something other than lowering prices that would increase your sales and/or increase profitability? This could include lowering costs, improving quality, improving customer service or revising your marketing strategy.

Increasing prices can be just as risky a strategy as lowering them. However, it may improve profitability even though your sales may decrease and it is this delicate balance between sales and profitability that you need to be aware of. The most important part of your plan to increase prices is how you inform your existing customers. No one wants to pay higher prices but there are ways to make price rises more acceptable:

- Explain the reasons behind the increase – if you are honest and reasonable then this can make it more tolerable and may even increase your customers' loyalty to your organisation.
- Send improved marketing materials to your customers along with the details of the price increase. Your aim here is to emphasise the benefits of your product or service.
- Relaunch the product. You can make changes to the product and then replace the old one with the revised one at a higher price. The production costs of the new product should preferably be cheaper, or at least the same, as the old one but the product be sufficiently different to be presented as a new product or an updated version.

Do you need to develop new products or services?

Making sure that you have the right product and that it continues to be needed by potential customers is a vital part of any marketing plan. Developing new products can be an expensive, risky process for any business but it is likely that sooner or later it will become a necessity. All products and services have a lifecycle and if any of yours are in the later stages of this cycle then you will need to develop new ones to ensure that your business prospers and continues to grow. The stages that all products have to go through – from initial development through to product decline are as follows:

- **Development** – this is when you develop the product or service and change it from an idea into something that is ready to offer to customers. Costs of research and development at this stage will be high.

- **Launch** – if you have got the product or service right then sales will grow rapidly from the launch and profits will be healthy. These profits should cover the extra marketing costs of the launch.
- **Growth** – at this point sales will be growing and you will be making money from the product or service. This is when you should be looking at reducing production costs to ensure profit levels can be maintained through the next phase. You should also be searching for new markets to extend the life of your product.
- **Plateau** – this is when sales have reached their peak and further growth is not possible. If you have brought down production costs as much as you can then it will be difficult to compete on price and to improve – or maintain – profit margins. It may be possible to extend the life of your product by adding new features or updating its design but developing new products should be your priority at this stage.
- **Decline** – this is when your product is, in effect, dying. Its performance is in decline, it faces competition from all sides, so prices are being driven down and it is very difficult, no matter how much marketing spend you throw at it, to increase sales.

As product decline appears to be inevitable, it is best if new products are continually in the pipeline. This will ensure that you will have products at different stages and so will have at least one at the peak of its profitability. It is also possible to extend the life of a product to a certain extent (though not indefinitely) by the use of the following means:

- More advertising – this will increase your marketing budget so you will need to be sure that the product's sales can be increased sufficiently to justify this.

- Looking for new markets for your product.
- Introducing minor additions to the product or updating the design to present it as a 'new' product.
- Finding different ways to sell the product.

All of these measures may extend the life of a product but will not prevent its sales decreasing indefinitely, so new products will always be necessary.

Let's look now at how you can get from having an idea for a new product to having something to offer to customers. As we've said, development and marketing costs of new products can be very high and there is always a risk as to the success of a product so there are a number of areas that you should consider to lessen this risk:

- Is there sufficient demand? To answer this question you obviously need to know your customers requirements. If in any doubt, you should talk to your customers and your salespeople and perhaps arrange a survey to confirm – or otherwise – that there is sufficient demand in the market to justify the development and marketing spend that will be necessary to get the product to market.
- Is it feasible? Can you produce it at a cost that will allow you to make a profit? Are you technically capable of producing it?
- Will it satisfy customers? This is linked to demand which we discussed above, but you should also ensure that the product will meet specific needs such as being easy to use, what benefits it will bring to customers and so on.
- Does it fit well with your business? Consider your goals and objectives. Any new product that you introduce to your business should further these goals and also fit into your product range.

If the answer to all these questions is a definite 'yes' then you can go ahead and develop your ideas further. Remember, a business will be more likely to remain profitable if there is a continual review and update of the products and services it offers, so the answer to the question, 'Do you need to develop new products or services?' is almost invariably 'yes'.

No matter how great the need for new products appears to be, it is important that costs are not allowed to get out of control. Don't try to introduce lots of new products at the same time. By phasing the development and introduction of new products, the costs will be spread over a manageable time period. You should also monitor the development carefully to 'weed out' things that are not working as planned before valuable resources are wasted. Remember that costs of developing new products can include:

- design costs
- new technology
- training
- staff
- materials
- market research – both internal and external costs
- increased overheads
- quality costs.

Case study

Two friends became business partners when they came up with an idea for a new kitchen gadget. Their company became very successful and they managed to get their clever gadget into national outlets. So, how did they develop their product and get it to the right market?

First, the pair of entrepreneurs spent many weeks researching the market. This included:

- obtaining market research reports
- consulting the relevant trade bodies and associations
- checking out all the main department stores and small cook shops to see what was available – there was nothing that did the same job
- getting advice from their local Chamber of Commerce
- conducting an on-street survey to see what the public thought of their product
- examining competitors' products that were available in a similar area (but not doing exactly the same job)
- checking out who the competitors sold their products to.

As a result of their extensive research they decided that there was a viable market for their product and that the best sales channel would be specialist kitchenware shops. They then had to set a price for their product and to do this they took into account:

- the prices being charged for competitors' products
- the costs of production, sales, marketing and delivery
- the fact that they should not set their price too low as they knew that it would be harder to raise it than to lower it if they had not got the price level quite right first time

They then developed their marketing plan. They found this the most difficult aspect of the product launch as their experience was concentrated in product design and logistics rather than sales and marketing. They therefore took advice from their

(Continued)

(Continued)

local Chamber of Commerce about how to put together a short but effective sales pitch. They practised delivering this until they were word perfect and could let a buyer know very quickly what they had to offer. They approached all the major kitchenware stockists and after some time and several visits and phone calls were successful with the first one that they had tried. They found that once they were accepted and stocked in one highly visible company, success with other companies became easier.

One important thing they learned was that nothing happens overnight. In their initial enthusiasm they had thought that within a year they would be showing a profit, but it took much longer than this. It took over 12 months of talking and negotiating with the first major chain that they approached before they got them to agree to stock the product. Added to the time they had spent already in developing the product, researching the market and sorting out the marketing, this meant that the product development and launch cycle eventually took nearly three years.

A good idea, well researched and getting help where it was needed resulted in a highly successful product launch.

Monitoring customer feedback

Monitoring everything you do is essential – if you don't take time to check that the plans you put in place are working you could miss opportunities to change and to be more successful. In the case of a marketing plan, not only will you have to monitor the progress of the actions within your organisation but also you will have to monitor how customers have received any changes you have made and the impact on your results. For example, are your staff implementing the changes as you planned them? Are your customers happy with the changes? Is the plan delivering its objectives?

Checking that everything is being implemented internally as you had planned will involve:

- regular review meetings with your team
- checking progress at key points within the plan
- being prepared to change your plan if unexpected difficulties are encountered
- taking remedial action where necessary.

Monitoring how your customers have reacted to the changes can be more difficult. You can, of course, commission a full-scale customer survey from a professional research company. This would need careful liaison with the company that you choose and you need to ensure that they ask the questions to which you need the answers. This solution would normally only be used in the case of a major product launch by a large organisation. If, however, your monitoring of customer feedback is to be done on a smaller, more personalised scale (i.e. internally), you need to consider the following:

- First, check information that you receive in the normal course of business – for example the number of customer complaints you receive, the amount of repeat orders, the number of new customers, number of sales enquiries and so on.
- Get staff who have customer contact on a regular basis to elicit comments from customers. This could include your sales force, call centre staff, telephonists, customer care assistants, engineers, repair staff and so on. You will need to put in place a system for capturing this information, but a quick question such as, 'What did you think of the new product launch?' or, 'How do you feel about the new complaints procedure?' can give you lots of valuable insight.

- Next, consider conducting your own customer survey. You could email or mail some or all of your customers asking them the questions to which you need to know the answers. This needs to be done with some caution as lengthy questionnaires or intrusive questioning can irritate some customers or may cause them to think that there is a problem in your organisation.

Whatever information you get back from your customers and from your staff, you need to be ready to act upon it. If the reaction is negative in any way or is not what you expected, you must take steps to correct it immediately. If you've changed an approach and customers don't like it, for example, you must ask yourself if the approach is right or wrong, whether it can be amended to make it more acceptable to your customers, whether it needs time for the customers to get used to it or if it does indeed need to be scrapped. This is a difficult decision and it should not be made in a hurry, but you should not hold on to an idea simply because it was your idea. Stubbornness will not win customers in this situation. You should also consider whether the change was communicated properly to your customers.

If, on the other hand, you get a positive reaction, then you should congratulate yourself and, above all, congratulate your team on their success.

Your final checkpoint in your evaluation of your marketing plan has to be a review of whether or not all the plan's objectives have been fully met. If the answer is yes, then you will need to recognise your team's achievements in some way and also to let any stakeholders know of the success. All the people who received a copy of the initial plan should also receive a copy of the full review, with their attention drawn to the meeting of the objectives.

SUMMARY

An essential part of a successful business is having the right product or service. As markets are continually changing it is important to keep what you are offering to customers under ongoing review. In this respect, it is vital that you thoroughly understand three things – your product, your customers' perceptions of it and what your competitors are offering.

In terms of your product you should understand its USP, what it can do, how it is made and the benefits it brings to your customers.

Your customers will see your product (or changes in it) differently to how you see it, so you will have to ask them what they think of it. This may entail a survey done by your own staff or by an independent market research agency if your budget allows for it. The advantages of this are that they will be able to give you a truer picture and an impartial, expert view. Choosing who to do this research for you involves a little research of your own first – you are looking for a researcher who has good references, is experienced, holds the appropriate licences and, of course, you can afford. Having chosen the agency you should brief them clearly about what you are trying to achieve. Then, whether you have conducted the survey yourself or paid an agency to do it for you, it is vital that you use the results to inform your marketing strategy.

Knowing what your competitors are doing is important. You can compare what you are doing with others in your field in order to see where you need to improve. Your competitors can also be a good source of ideas. Again, this will require a lot of research so that you are able to compare products, prices and customer perceptions.

A SWOT (Strengths, Weaknesses, Opportunities and Threats) analysis will give you the last piece of the puzzle in understanding whether or not you have the right product or service. *(Continued)*

(Continued)

Having done all this research and analysis, you will need to use all the information to revise your marketing strategy. It will allow you to set objectives, decide what needs to be done and who will do it, communicate the strategy to all involved and then review your plans regularly.

We then looked briefly at how to write a marketing plan and at the stages of the life of a product – from development, through its launch, the growth phase, plateau and the decline. As all products go through these stages it is vital that new products are always being planned. In developing a product the risks must be assessed – is there sufficient demand, will it satisfy customers, does it fit with the business?

Finally, we looked at the need to monitor feedback on new products. We need to check that everything is going to plan internally, and also monitor customer reactions by checking the information available – for example, the number of complaints received – and by keeping in regular contact with customers. Again, it is vital that we act on the information we receive.

ACTION CHECKLIST

1. Write a description of one of the products or services produced by your organisation. Include how it is made and what it does.
2. Find a USP for this product.
3. List three features of the product then convert them to benefits that the product would give to customers.
4. Analyse which stage in its lifecycle this product is at.
5. Conduct a SWOT analysis of your organisation.

10

What does it take to generate sales?

Sales are the life-blood of most businesses, so it is worth taking some time to understand the various ways in which they can be generated, even if selling is not specifically part of your work role. The ability to sell, whether it is a product or an idea, is an essential skill in any manager. In this chapter we will look at how to find sales leads, how to match what you are offering to what the buyer needs, how to prepare a sales proposal and how to close a sale.

Identifying sales opportunities

Finding new sales is essential to all profit-making organisations. It is proven that you will lose approximately 10 per cent of your existing sales each year. This may be because of your customers going out of business, changing markets, changes within your organisation or the changing requirements of your customers. Whatever the reason, you must replace those sales – and more – if your company is to survive. Even in the case of non-profit-making organisations, such as charities, there is a continual need to find new sources of revenue as the old ones decrease or disappear.

The first thing to do is to examine thoroughly your current customer records. Can you sell more – either more of the same or perhaps different products – to these customers? Analyse what these customers have bought in the past and when. If you can see patterns such as a quarterly or monthly order, consider putting in place a system whereby you contact these customers on a regular basis to ask them for an order. If you present this as an extra service to save them the trouble of contacting you, then you will be developing closer relationships with your customers. It will also give you a better chance of selling more to them and lessen the chance of your losing the business to a competitor. If you're in regular contact with your customers there are numerous benefits for you.

There is a lot of information contained in the sales data your company will keep on a regular basis and it is important that you use it effectively. Look at what sorts of organisations are included in your existing customer list. If you take note of what sector your customers are in, what size of companies are there and their location, this will give you plenty of clues as to how you can expand your customer base.

To keep a supply of new customers coming into your company you will also have to generate plenty of sales leads. This can be done in a number of ways:

- Ask your existing customers for referrals. They know the value of your product and the service that you give – or they wouldn't be your customers – so make sure that you take advantage of their knowledge. They will know their sector of the market and it is likely that organisations similar to theirs are ideal potential customers for you.
- Search in the local press. Even if you have an international market for your products, you will probably be able to find new leads in your local area. Look at news

articles about start-up companies, advertisements for job vacancies that might hint at expansion, or at least a thriving company – just the sort of organisation to approach in your sales efforts.

- Network – attending networking events will broaden your local knowledge and you will make plenty of new contacts that can be turned into sales.
- Get to know your local area. Just by being out and about – and keeping your eyes open – you can find leads. Try a walk around a commercial or industrial area.
- Use the internet – search for organisations that are in the same field as your best customers or in the area into which you want to expand.
- Take part in local events such as jobs fairs and conferences.
- Don't forget your local library – they usually have a selection of directories and trade magazines from which you can make note of companies in the sector you are researching.

As you accumulate leads you will need to be organised about how you keep their details in a useable format. There will be details such as addresses, telephone numbers, website addresses and the name of the person to contact. It is also useful to keep as much information about the business as possible, such as type and size of business. There are several software systems that will help with this contact management and also offer efficient ways to track the activity when you are following up these leads.

When you have identified a number of prospects you should do some research before you approach them. Obviously, you will need to know plenty about their business and why they need what you have to offer (see Chapter 3), as this will also apply to your prospects, but you should also consider why they are not currently buying from your organisation. Find out who their current supplier is and if they have any concerns or areas of discontent with this supplier. Can you identify any advantages for the prospect of buying from you instead of their current supplier?

Making sales appointments

Your next step will be to approach your potential customers. Your aim should be to get face-to-face with the people in your list who you have identified as being possible users of your products or services. There is a variety of ways to do this:

In writing

This can be by letter, perhaps enclosing a brochure or other product information, or by email. All unsolicited written communications must be kept short and you need to grab attention quickly – before the email is deleted or the letter hits the bin. For a letter this means giving it a heading that stands out and gives the recipient a reason to read on. The same applies to emails, except that this heading will go in the subject line. Including customer testimonials with written approaches to potential customers is often effective. Remember that any written approach you make will always have to be followed up by phone to check that it got to the right person and to get their reaction to it.

By telephone

This is a good way of making the initial contact with your prospective buyer, but it requires plenty of preparation and is often viewed as little more than a 'numbers game' – the more calls you make the greater your chance of success will be. When you pick up the phone to make your sales calls you must be ready to deliver a short but effective summary of what you have to offer – no more than about 30 seconds. Make sure that you deliver your pitch to the right person rather than the receptionist or someone who will routinely reject sales calls. You can increase your chances of success by asking for the correct person by name even before you announce your own name or company. You will need to be persistent.

In person

Visiting the business premises without an appointment rarely works in large organisations and very few people who have the authority to sign an order will have sufficient spare time in their working day to see anyone who casually calls into their offices. However, it can be a good way of obtaining information and it may work more often with smaller organisations. The important thing is to be prepared with the name of the person you want to see and a short version of what you are offering. Many of the points about cold calling by telephone also apply when you call in person.

INSTANT TIP

The most important thing about getting a sales appointment is that it must be with the right person. Part of your sales lead research should be to find the name of the person in the organisation you are targeting who has the authority to make buying decisions for your type of product or service.

When you've made your sales appointments you must prepare yourself thoroughly for the meeting. Obviously, you must know your own products and services inside out. You need to know how they can be of benefit to your potential customer and to be able to answer any objections and questions with confidence. You also need to know quite a bit about the organisation you are visiting so check out their website, look at any advertising they are doing, including locally in the jobs market, find out who their customers are, the size of their business and how they are viewed in their sector, for example, are they market leaders? Are they well respected? Are they thought of as old-fashioned or go-ahead? All of this will help you to tailor your offer to their specific needs and will also make the meeting easier in that you will be able to speak knowledgably about their business. Imagine how difficult a meeting would become if your potential customer informed you that it was well known in the market that they were pulling out of the sector, making your offer out of place and irrelevant! You will also need to know your competitors. If you don't understand exactly what you are competing against, you will not be able to make your offer stand out from the competition. At this point you will have the basis for a plan for the meeting – questions to ask, points to make and so on.

Sales presentations

You can now turn to the sales presentation itself. Again this needs plenty of preparation to make it work and also to make yourself comfortable in what can be a very challenging situation. The better your preparation, the easier the meeting will be. Apart from researching your prospect as outlined above, you should consider:

- Who will the meeting be with? How many people will be present and what will their priorities be (Financial

Directors, for example, may have different priorities from those of a Production Manager)?

- Will it be a formal meeting or a quick, informal chat?
- What are your objectives for the meeting? Are you planning to get a signed order or simply to introduce your company as a first step in what you know will be a lengthy process? Will you need to set up a further meeting with other people from your potential customer's organisation?
- A list of questions that you will need to ask to be sure of what the requirements are.
- Think about the possible objections that could be raised and prepare answers.
- Be clear about how you will introduce your organisation and its products.
- What are the key benefits of your product or service?
- Will there be facilities for the use of presentation technology? If so, you will need to be sure that you're sufficiently rehearsed to deliver an effective presentation. It is becoming increasingly important for a salesperson to be able to use a variety of methods to enhance their presentation. These include laptop presentations (usually using PowerPoint™ software), professionally made DVDs, transparencies, and flipcharts. All of these require preparation and careful thought as to when they will be appropriate. A general rule is to use them only when the presentation will be enhanced by their use and to become thoroughly familiar with their use before trying them out on real customers.

> ## INSTANT TIP
>
> View your presentation materials from a similar position to the one that your audience will be in – not just as you're sitting at your computer. You need to be sure that the graphics and font size are easily viewed from a distance. Timing is important too so have a complete run through before the day.

Does your product match your prospect's needs?

An important part of any sales meeting is matching your product to the potential customer's needs. First you will have to find out exactly what these needs are. Of course, you wouldn't have made the appointment if you didn't think the organisation could benefit from your product and your prospect probably would not have agreed to see you without some knowledge of your organisation and its products, but you should not assume too much. You need to ascertain the buyer's views and requirements. With careful questioning you should be able to find out what the buyer's expectations and priorities are and what gaps there are, if any, in the service or product that they are currently buying and price indications. Try to find out more about the company at this stage too, to add to the research you will have done prior to the meeting. Careful questioning should be matched with careful listening – so make sure you allow the buyer to talk.

When you have elicited the information you need about their requirements you must match their needs with your product offer. You may have prepared a basic preparation built upon your product and what companies usually expect from it but you must always tailor your approach and presentation to the specific needs of the person and company to which you are presenting. For example, if your product has a long shelf life but you have found out that your potential customer turns around all supplies very quickly then there is little point in emphasising the long-term nature of your product, but if you have found that they require a wide variety of sizes of the product and you are able to offer this then bring that into the presentation and highlight this throughout. While doing this it is effective to repeat back the buyer's comments on these points to emphasise the match between his requirements and your product offer.

Addressing objections

Handling objections during a sales presentation is a critical part of the sales process. Of course, you should have been able to rule out some objections with the preparation you have done prior to the sales meeting, such as researching your potential customer's business, thinking of possible objections and covering those matters in your presentation, but there will usually be something brought up by the buyer during the presentation that you will have to deal with and overcome if you are to achieve a sale.

INSTANT TIP

If a buyer raises an objection, do not show any sign of irritation or worry – simply make a mental or written note of the issue and deal with it later in the meeting.

In dealing with any objection you should first establish that it is a genuine objection. Sometimes a buyer will raise an issue to stall for time or because he or she does not really want to change suppliers

– even if they can see the advantages of doing so – because change can be threatening. You can start to do this by clarifying exactly what the issue is. Ask questions and note the answers. If it is something about your product or organisation that is a real stumbling block preventing your customer deciding to buy, then you will need to find a solution. Remember that an objection is often a sign of interest – the buyer genuinely wants information to enable him to buy. You then have a number of options to try to overcome the objection:

- Ask the buyer if he or she is in a position to give you the order if you can solve this one problem – this will ensure that you are not solving one problem simply to be faced with another. It will clarify that this is indeed a genuine objection. This is a further opportunity to be sure that the person you are dealing with is the right person – the one with the authority to place an order – and to avoid wasting time dealing with someone who cannot or will not buy.
- Explain to the buyer how your product can solve the problem or how you can structure the sale to ensure that his or her fears are overcome.
- Agree a compromise – an 'if I give this, can you do that' type of response.
- Call someone at your office to find an answer to his or her query.
- Make a sale conditional on your meeting the requirements.
- Agree a further meeting when you will have the answer to the problem.

Of course, your aim in all of this is not only to end the meeting with a sale but also with a happy, satisfied customer.

Closing in a win-win situation

If you have handled all the buyer's objections in a competent and professional manner and are happy that he or she is interested, then getting the order may be a straightforward way to end the meeting. Alternatively, you may have come to the conclusion that, for whatever reason, this buyer is unlikely ever to buy your product and it may well be that this is outside your control. In these cases the sales meeting will come to a natural end.

INSTANT TIP

Try a 'trial close' to see if the buyer is ready to buy or if there is more work to do. You could ask, 'Are you ready to discuss a deal?' or, 'Shall we move on to discussing the detail?' This may result in bringing the order a step closer or it may reveal further objections that can be dealt with when they are out in the open.

However, it may be that at this stage there is still some doubt in the buyer's mind and it is then that a salesperson will need to work hard. To close the sale he or she will use a closing technique such as:

- **Ask for the go ahead** – politely but firmly ask for the buyer's commitment.
- **Alternative close** – ask a question giving alternative answers (both of which would mean an order was forthcoming). For example, 'Would you like that in green or red?' or, 'Would the large or small pack size suit you?'
- **Assumption close** – this assumes that the order is 'in the bag' and is usually a question clarifying some detail of the order such as, 'Are you looking for a quick delivery?'

Which of these techniques a salesperson chooses to use will depend on how the sales meeting has gone so far. There may have been objections raised, but if these have been dealt with as the meeting has gone along, then the salesperson will be in a position to assess how likely the buyer is to place an order and will have spotted 'buying signals' or signs that there are genuine objections. The salesperson will need to watch out for the buyer's body language – such as nodding in agreement or looking bored.

There will be times, however, when a genuine objection is raised that the salesperson cannot answer at the time. There are three options when this happens:

1. Arrange a further meeting with a promise to bring all the relevant information.
2. Call someone back at the office to get an answer.
3. Try to make an agreement subject to getting the answer that the buyer wants.

When the main objection is price it can be tempting to lower your prices in a bid to get a quick sale. However, a good salesperson will always consider the long-term effect of lowering prices. You should keep the bottom line in mind as lowering prices may result in the sale becoming unprofitable and affect your organisation's capacity to maintain the quality of the product or the customer service. It is worth trying to restate the benefits and make your case for why the product is worth the asking price. However, if price really is a stumbling block, there are still a few options to consider:

- Offer a discount if the customer will increase the order quantity.
- Agree to a lower price for a different product or aspect of the service. It may be that you could change the product to make it less expensive to produce or that you have an

alternative, cheaper product to offer. You may be able to take the order on at a reduced price if you can choose when to deliver, thereby using a quiet time to produce the goods perhaps.

- Reduce the price by a very small amount – and slowly – insisting that this is the best you can do without affecting the product.

Depending on how the meeting goes, it may be possible to make a sale. However, it may be that the salesperson will assess the situation and feel that, although a sale may not be made on the day, the buyer is interested, so decide to offer to send a quotation that will clarify the product offer. It is important that an appointment is also made at this time to discuss the proposal and, hopefully, to close the sale at that second meeting. There will be more in the next section about how to put a sales proposal together.

INSTANT TIP

Ask for the order! More business is lost by not asking for the order than from genuine objections. Don't do all the work then not close the sale in the right way.

What to include in a sales proposal

A written sales proposal may be prepared before a sales appointment if the potential customer has made an enquiry, but they are usually prepared following sales visits to confirm what has been agreed. This is where you formalise the sale, and care must be taken to include the various items that your organisation has committed to:

- The price – this should be stated clearly and prominently.
- What the price covers – does it include delivery or is that an extra cost? Exactly how many – and of what – are included in the price?
- The validity of the quotation – if you are able to hold the quoted price for six months, then say so. This saves confusion if the buyer does not place an order for some time after the quotation and by that time your costs have increased. No quotation is valid forever, so specify limits.
- Order fulfilment details – when will the goods or service be supplied and how.
- The payment terms that will apply to an order. Agreeing them now will save putting your organisation in the position of having to bargain when an order is placed. This would put you in the weak position of being in danger of losing the order if you do not agree to terms that are not really acceptable to you.
- Contact details for your organisation – what should the buyer do if they have a query? Give contact details for the people who will be able to answer questions – or take an order – from the potential customer.

As you can see, the purpose of the sales proposal is not just to advise or confirm a price. It must also make clear all the details that may impact on any order you may receive.

Finally, remember that the sale is not complete until you have delivered the order and have been paid for it. Even then, it is worth keeping in touch with the customer to demonstrate the superior customer service that your organisation offers and answer any queries your customer may have, and also to make sure you are in touch when another order is due.

Sales via the internet

Although most sales for the majority of organisations will come via personal contact in sales meetings or by telephone, the internet is a good source of sales for many companies now and is becoming an increasingly important way to generate sales. Obviously, your website is the most important aspect of this sales stream and a professionally designed and built website is usually the best way to go for most organisations of any size. Most people are unable to influence their organisation's website, but if this falls within your remit, when planning a website to achieve online sales you should keep the following in mind:

- Make an impact with your home page. This is, in effect, your shop window so it needs to invite people into the site to discover more about what you're offering.
- Make it easy to get around. Your website must be user-friendly as customers will quickly give up and move on to another website if they find they are waiting too long for graphics to load or if they find it confusing as to what they have to do to place an order or find a specific item.
- Use plenty of photos. Most people do not want to read blocks of text on a website and, as they say, a picture paints a thousand words. Bear in mind that your buyers will not be able to touch the products or to ask questions so photos are invaluable in displaying your products.
- Make sure the site is secure – and that you tell your potential customers that it is secure. Buyers will not be willing to part with their financial and personal details if they have any doubts about the security of their credit card details, for example, or how you will use – and store – any personal details that you may ask for.
- Don't forget that any visitors to your website can just as easily visit your competitors' websites so it is likely that

they will compare your prices and what you are offering with others available online. Checking out the competition's online presence is essential when setting up your own website.

● Be aware that your audience online will be much wider than your usual customer base. This might mean that you have to alter your approach if you are used to presenting yourself as a local company, for example, or you might need to consider presenting the site in different languages if you are aiming at overseas sales.

When you've set up your website, the address must be publicised as widely and as often as possible. It should appear on every piece of written information that your company produces. This includes letterheads, emails, business cards, brochures, leaflets, invoices, compliment slips and in every item that appears in the press. If the local paper – or even a national newspaper – runs an item on your organisation, make sure that your website address appears at the end of the article. In fact, make your new website into a news item – let your local newspapers know about your launch and let all your customers and suppliers know that you're offering a new facility for them. To enable potential new customers to find your website you will probably need to pay for search engine optimisation so that your website appears high up in the rankings when certain terms are entered in search engines.

SUMMARY

In this chapter we have looked at what it takes to generate sales for your organisation. Because there is a continual need to find new customers as existing ones go out of business or change their suppliers, this process of generating sales leads and increasing sales must be an ongoing process.

First you should consider if and how you can sell more to existing customers, then look at ways to generate sales leads by, for example, referrals, using local information, networking, via the internet and attending events such as conferences in your market area.

We saw that your next step is to find a way to get in front of your prospective customers to present your products or services. Sales appointments and presentations must be carefully prepared for by arming yourself or your sales staff with a good product and company knowledge, setting objectives for the meeting and thinking about possible objections and the answers to them. Your next step is to match your product to the customer's needs by finding out exactly what they are and then tailoring your approach accordingly.

We then looked at how to get an order at a sales meeting or presentation by using one of a variety of suggested 'closes' – asking for the order, the alternative close and the assumptive close.

Next we looked at what a sales proposal should include – price details, terms and conditions, validity of the quote, delivery and payment terms, plus full contact details to respond to the proposal.

Finally, we looked at selling via the internet. This entails setting up a website (or checking your existing website's suitability). It should have impact right from the start, be user-friendly, well illustrated and secure. This last point should be made obvious to customers so that fear of fraud will not hold them back from making a purchase. The content of a website should be suitable for all possible markets including, if necessary, text in more than one language to cater for overseas customers. Of course, no matter how good your website is it will not bring sales unless people can find it so its address must be well publicised and search engine optimisation should be considered.

ACTION CHECKLIST

1. Consider how you would generate ten new sales leads for your company – this may be through contacts of your own or from things you have seen in the local press, for example.

2. Prepare yourself for an imaginary sales presentation (unless of course, this is part of your job, in which case it can be a genuine sales presentation).

3. Devise questions for an alternative close and an assumptive close for products or services that your organisation offers.

4. Find one or two sales proposals that the sales department of your organisation have recently sent out and assess whether they include all the necessary details. Could they be improved?

5. Check out your organisation's website from a sales point of view. Is it user-friendly, does it cover all the possible markets for your product or service, is it easy to find if you don't have the address?

How can you improve performance in your organisation?

Key management challenges of improving organisational performance

One of the main problems in improving performance is finding management time to do it. While things are going well, the business is profitable and there are no major problems, it is tempting for everyone to carry on doing what they're doing. Keeping a company on the track that has been established is a difficult, time-consuming task and it can seem impossible for a manager to set time aside to review performance and instigate changes to improve it. Conversely, if things are going badly everyone's time will be taken up with fire-fighting, so making major changes is probably not on the list of things to do. However, it is essential in managing a business to conduct regular reviews. Are you still following the direction that was decided on when the current goals and objectives were set? After a thorough review of performance it will probably be found that there is a need to make improvements and possibly even change direction.

During this review process it will be necessary to examine every area of the business, looking particularly at the following aspects:

- **What the organisation does** – are the products and services still right for the market? There will have been changes in the market since the last review (or since the business was set up if this is the first review) and the products must change to accommodate these changes.
- **Successes** – what is the organisation's most successful product? Knowing what works is important so that everyone can keep doing it and perhaps do more of the same. It is necessary to learn from successes as well as from failures.
- **Failures** – what is the least successful product? It may be decided to drop this product from your range or maybe revamp it so that it can be re-launched.
- **Costs** – can a better deal be gained from the organisation's suppliers or different materials or types of products used?
- **Staffing levels** – does the organisation have the right number of staff in the right areas? Are some areas struggling to keep up while others appear over-staffed?
- **Customer service** – is the organisation still satisfying its customers or are there signs of problems here?

Of course, this sort of performance review will take time and it may be necessary to carry out quite a bit of research but that should not be allowed to intervene. It is a vital task if the organisation is to remain viable. It is likely that this will not be a one-person exercise in anything apart from the very smallest of organisations, so it will probably be necessary to enlist support from the financial people and senior staff from all departments.

A key change that can be made that will greatly assist is to constantly show that management are behind the need to improve the performance of the organisation and are 'doing their bit'. They must demonstrate clearly to all the organisation's employees (plus customers and suppliers where possible) that they are committed to continual improvement and have made the time, money and other necessary resources available to make it work. This commitment must be long term. This can be demonstrated by the development of a well-planned strategy that has the necessary resources allocated to it and involves everyone in the organisation.

Another vital element of a move towards continual improvement is to ensure that there is a culture shift. It needs to become second nature to everyone in the organisation. This requires continual communication at all levels. This could take the form of regular meetings for everyone involved, smaller team meetings to discuss and decide specific improvements within departments, newsletters, team briefings, and informal meetings such as a senior manager checking in with a junior manager at their desk. It should be noted that although informal meetings are a valuable addition to communication there should be a plan to communicate essential information on a regular basis via formal means to ensure that everyone in the organisation has at least the basics of what is going on communicated to them.

Set the standards

Setting standards to be met in the organisation is an important way of improving performance. Targets are a way of making sure that the strategy of the organisation is translated into measures that everyone can understand.

The first question to be asked here is, 'What should we measure?' The answer to this question could be different according to what drives the business, but one factor that is the same for all measures is that they must be quantifiable. This does not mean that it is only possible to measure financial information – although these will undoubtedly form a major part of the business performance indicators – but must also include important items such as the standard of the organisation's customer service. As we discussed earlier, this aspect of the business can be measured in a number of ways, including how many complaints are received from customers or the amount of faulty goods that are returned, in addition to less tangible measures such as staff attitudes and behaviour. To find the best targets for the organisation it will be necessary to know what drives the success of the business. For example, the business might be competing in a market that is price-driven. In this case, costs will be a driver of the organisation's success. If the organisation is producing high-end, expensive products, then it is likely that quality will be far more important. If senior managers have difficulty finding all the drivers of the business, it is a good idea to go back to the organisation's long-term strategy. What was its main thrust as regards making a profit? An examination of these ideas should result in a better understanding of the drivers of your organisation's success.

Having identified these drivers you will need to decide how to measure performance in these areas. Finding the measure that will accurately show your progress in a specific area will give vital information that can be used to produce continual improvement in the organisation.

Back in Chapter 5 we looked at setting KPIs in the area of customer service. If this is important to your business – as it is in most organisations – then setting standards here would be the ideal way to start. These will give performance targets that will drive improvements in just the right area for your organisation. As you may recall, it is important that KPIs are quantifiable so that any vagueness and inconsistency are eliminated.

Checking your organisation's performance against the standards that have been set will produce information about how the organisation's performance is changing and will let management manage performance.

Collecting information about your ongoing performance

The area that has been selected to concentrate on in terms of performance targets will dictate how the information is collected. So, for example, if data is being collected about employee performance then it will be necessary to use both quantitative information, such as profit per employee, and qualitative information, such as the results of staff appraisals. Of course, a lot of the information needed will already be there in financial reports or data produced on a routine basis by the organisation's internal computer programs. This includes profit margins, cash flow and turnover in the accounting area, plus sales data, complaints information in the customer service area, and lots of information that relates to manufacturing, such as goods produced per hour per employee or stock turnover.

The information to be collected will be determined, as we have said, by what it has been decided are the key drivers of success and the manager or team carrying out the task will need to have a thorough understanding of the areas of the business that come into this category. Collecting the data will greatly assist this understanding.

It should be noted that there is a wide variety of computing software that will help in collecting and analysing vast quantities of information about the business. This can be tailored to suit the individual organisation's requirements. Much of this is accounting-based but there is a wide variety of areas that can be measured and if the data that would be produced is likely to be unmanageable, then it is worthwhile considering investing in software to help.

Benchmarking

All businesses need to set the standards that they are aiming for with Key Performance Indicators. These will help them see how to improve their performance. Benchmarking, however, is more than setting internal standards – it is about making comparisons. These are usually with other businesses operating in the same business sector, but sometimes benchmarking is carried out between different departments of one business. For the purposes of this book we will concentrate on benchmarking against other businesses.

The things that are chosen to measure and benchmark will, as with internal improvements, depend on the areas of the business that are considered to be most important in driving the business and the emphasis here may change from time to time. However, the key aspects that are benchmarked most often include:

- **Profitability** – the performance indicators that can be benchmarked in the area of profitability include the gross and net profit margins, the return on capital employed and the operating margin.
- **Accounting ratios** – these include gearing, liquidity and efficiency ratios.
- **Cash flow** – the input and output of cash is an important indicator of the condition of a business.
- **Manufacturing performance** – there are lots of ways to measure the manufacturing process, including output per employee or per worker hour, stock turnover, quantity of faulty goods produced or the amount of orders delivered on time.
- **Staff performance** – this could include sales or profit per employee.

Here we're looking specifically at improving customer service so the most useful measures to benchmark in this area include:

- what proportion of orders are repeat business
- length of order-to-delivery cycle
- number of complaints from customers
- quantity of returned goods.

Of course, it is not necessary to benchmark all of these measures at one time. The task is to find one – or perhaps two – of these performance indicators that best measures the area of the business where improvement is required.

Although it should be relatively easy to establish benchmark figures for one's own organisation, it is more difficult to find equivalent data for other businesses. This sort of information is usually obtained from market reports that can be bought according to market sector. Alternatively, organisations such as trade associations and Chambers of Commerce may be able to help to establish appropriate data.

When two sets of benchmarking data have been obtained, then the person or team responsible will be able to set benchmark values in the area where improvement is required. These values can then be used to set targets along the way to reaching new goals.

Creating an improvement culture

The key to successful performance improvement lies in developing an improvement culture that is evident throughout the entire organisation. Two essential elements in this are the setting of targets and getting employees to buy in to the idea of improvement.

When setting targets, it is vital that the staff who have to meet them fully understand what is expected of them and that they agree to them. It is a common mistake in businesses for management to set targets that are perfectly achievable but for them to retain ownership of the targets and to take on responsibility for meeting those targets. This leaves employees feeling that the targets are being imposed, have nothing really to do with them and that the targets are probably unachievable anyway. In order to foster a culture of improvement that will be successful, it is necessary to involve all members of staff fully. This can be done in a number of ways:

● Explain what the management is trying to achieve. Ensure that everyone understands the objective and why improvements are necessary. This can be done in individual meetings or as a group, but care should be taken to allow time for problems to be aired by staff and for them to ask questions. It should be possible to determine, from questions asked and comments made, whether they have fully understood what management is trying to achieve.
● Gain agreement right from the start.
● Ask staff for their input. If they are doing a job they will usually have ideas about how it could be done better.
● Discuss employees' ideas with them in detail. Find out why they feel improvements are necessary. Everyone adapts to change better if they feel it was their idea and this can work very well when trying to improve performance within organisations.
● Make resources available to put employee ideas into action. This could be as simple as rearranging their work so that they have time allocated to concentrate on meeting the targets, or it could involve expenditure on software for example.

- Foster a team spirit by setting group targets as well as individual targets.
- Consider breaking targets down into weekly objectives. For example, they may have been set a target of increasing sales by 10 per cent over the year, but it is preferable if staff are shown how this can be done. A weekly target of five extra sales appointments or a specified number of new contacts may be what will achieve the annual target.
- Set up regular meetings after targets have been set. These should be used to discuss how things are going and how things could be changed rather than just to check that staff are meeting targets. Make sure these meetings are held frequently enough so that employees do not feel that they have been given targets then abandoned.

An area often neglected when trying to change the culture of an organisation is that of induction training. However, this is a relatively easy area to change and can be very effective. The aim is for induction training to include a section devoted to ensuring that the values of an organisation and its strategy are communicated to all new employees. When this has been developed, it can be a good idea to let all existing staff have access to the material – perhaps with some adaptation.

Implementing improvements

The implementation of changes is covered in various sections of this book. Suffice it to say here that the key actions necessary to achieve improvement – along with the required outcomes and the deadlines for the improvements to be achieved – should be communicated clearly to the members of staff who will have responsibility for making things happen. It will then be possible to assign targets and responsibilities to the key players and they, in turn, will be able to set objectives for their own teams.

Measuring improvements

Using your KPIs to pinpoint improvements is vital to a business but it should be remembered that they can also help to predict problems. Here we will focus on using your measures to improve performance. So, how will KPIs work in the various areas of the business? Let's look at three specific areas as examples.

Customer retention

Here the KPIs will probably be based on data that has been collected giving details of the proportion of sales that is from repeat orders (i.e. sales to existing customers) and from measures relating to customer service (such as the length of your order fulfilment cycle, the number of complaints received and how quickly the phone is answered in the customer service department). So, for example, if it has been found that one of the reasons that customers have been lost in the past is because it has taken too long to send out the goods ordered, then the relevant KPI will be based on shortening the length of time taken from receipt of order to dispatch. It might have been found that it currently takes 40 days and management has decided that 30 days would improve customer retention (a month being what customers have advised is the maximum they find acceptable, for example). The target then to achieve within six months is 30 days for the order-to-delivery cycle. Having explained these findings, gained agreement from the staff involved and obtained their ideas as to how this can be achieved, this could be broken down into monthly or even weekly targets for the team. Of course, to achieve an improvement like this it will first be necessary to understand fully what is causing the problem and, again, the staff in the department are likely to have some, if not all, of the answers.

Costs reduction

Here again management should follow the path of consulting staff for the reasons behind the problem and for their input into what can be improved and how. In this situation attention will be focused mainly on purchasing or manufacturing staff if a reduction in the cost of producing the goods is required. A reduction in these costs may enable the organisation to sell the products at a lower price in order to make it more competitive or simply increase profitability. If it has been decided that this is a KPI for your business then this must be made very clear to employees – especially the ones who will have to achieve the targets that have been set.

Reducing returned goods

This KPI will be aimed at improving customer service and will also produce the benefit of reducing the costs associated with receiving returned goods and replacing them, and the administrative costs. Of course, to get to the root of the problem it is necessary to understand why the goods are being returned. Here customer service staff will probably have many of the answers because customers will have told them, but it is also useful for management to conduct their own research with customers so that what is needed to reduce the volume of returned goods can be fully understood.

In all of these situations it will be necessary to establish exactly what the current position is and then measure the equivalent results at set intervals. It is always better to agree these intervals and methods of measurement with the staff involved.

Case study

The MD of a software development company used KPIs to help him achieve his business goals. The main aim was to increase new business.

The first step was to conduct a thorough review of the business. This showed that there were many encouraging aspects of the business – staff were well-qualified technically and very motivated, they had a good reputation in their market for top-quality products and for customer service. However, it was found that repeat business was decreasing steadily. Further investigation showed that price pressure was the principal reason behind the falling order book and that larger firms were undercutting their prices.

Following extensive consultation in which the new goals for the business were explained, monthly targets were set for increased volumes of repeat business and also for each salesperson to gain new customers. These were broken down further into weekly targets for the number of sales calls that each member of the sales department had to make to prospective customers and the number of client visits that each salesperson had to make was also carefully targeted.

Following the introduction of these new targets, the results were closely monitored in both formal and informal meetings. These gave members of staff the opportunity to report and discuss their results and for management to find out any barriers to the success of their plans. These meetings were also used to set weekly targets based on the previous week's results so that the approach was constantly tailored to what happened from week to week. The staff found this a useful approach in that they had frequent opportunities to express concerns or to report success and to get help with the detail of their jobs while the management were able to monitor results and adjust their approach.

A real effort was also made to include the members of the sales team in the discussions that took place on a regular basis so that they felt that they owned the targets and were making a real contribution to the efforts to resolve the problem with a solution they understood and supported.

After six months the downward trend of repeat business had been halted and within a year there was an upward trend for orders received from existing customers as well as many new enquiries coming into the company from prospective customers with many of these being converted into customers.

SUMMARY

In this chapter we addressed the question of improving performance and noted that continual improvement is essential in any organisation. Regular reviews must be conducted.

First we looked at setting standards so that the organisation's strategy is translated into measures that everyone can understand and work towards. To do this it is first necessary to collect information about the organisation's current performance – both tangible aspects such as financial information and also the less tangible areas such as customer and staff perceptions.

At this point we also looked at benchmarking – comparing the organisation's performance against other organisations

(Continued)

(Continued)

operating in a similar market area. We concentrated on a key aspect – customer service. Internal information can then be compared with data gained from an external market report.

Next we looked at how to create an improvement culture within the organisation. This involves giving clear explanations to staff of what management is trying to achieve, getting agreement and input from them, discussing their ideas in detail and then setting group targets to encourage a team spirit. This should be backed up with the necessary resources.

We then touched briefly on how to implement the changes and on how to measure the resulting improvements. Here, we concentrated on three specific areas – customer retention, reducing costs and reducing the amount of returned goods – using KPIs to measure the improvements in these important areas.

ACTION CHECKLIST

1. Name three tangible and three less tangible areas of performance in your organisation that could be improved.
2. How would you set targets for each of these areas?
3. Explain how you would go about making improvements in these areas.
4. Consider targets you have personally been set. Are they annual targets? If so, break them down into weekly targets. Do you think that this make them more achievable?
5. Apart from measuring improvements, how else can KPIs be used to affect an organisation's performance?

12

The Companion Interview: Ruth Spellman on Getting Results

The following interview with Ruth Spellman OBE was conducted by Hodder Education in September 2009, just as the Chartered Management Institute (CMI) prepared to re-brand.

As chief executive of the CMI, Ruth Spellman OBE leads the drive to encourage individuals, businesses and government to invest in the high level skills we need to increase UK competitiveness and productivity.

Prior to joining the Institute in June 2008, Ruth was the first female chief executive officer of the Institution of Mechanical Engineers, following seven successful years as Chief Executive of Investors in People. Prior to that she was a senior member of the consulting practice at Coopers and Lybrand, HR Director of the NSPCC and an adviser to NEDO (the National Economic Development Office). She brings a broad experience of the private, public and voluntary sectors to her new role and offers a fascinating insight into how best to get results in any sector.

Ruth was awarded an OBE in the 2007 New Year Honours List for services to Workplace Learning.

Your career has been spent mainly in the so-called not for profit sector. Do you think there is a distinctive approach to achieving results in that particular sector or do you see the challenges as essentially the same as the commercial sector? And do you think that in fact the measures i.e. the way you measure results, are the same in the two sectors as well?

Well, I have in fact worked in all three sectors. So I started off in the City as a trainee investment analyst. Then I worked for a nationalised industry – the coal industry at a very difficult time in its history when there were lots of disputes going on. Following that I worked in the public sector as a civil servant, then for Coopers and Lybrand in the private sector – that's as private sector as you can get! Then I moved on to work in the not-for-profit sector. So it wasn't until the 1990s that I started with a not-for-profit organisation. This was first as HR director at the NSPCC and then as CEO of Investors in People, followed by the Institution of Mechanical Engineers and then here at the CMI. So it's very much a mixed career, a mixed portfolio-type career.

Which I think is very typical, actually, of people of my generation; there wasn't a linear career for women particularly, it was very much going into those positions that were interesting and actually trying to mix and match my experience against different requirements. So I do think there are some different emphases in the not-for-profit sector. We do have to relate to people's values and do that as directly as we can. Don't make an apology for it. Acknowledge that you are working for a value-based organisation but then I think really understand and work with those values. To do some things which the voluntary sector is not very good at, which is to focus on the efficiencies. Really, just because you've got good values that doesn't let you off on the commercial disciplines. I think what I would like to see is that respect for the values woven in with really effective and efficient working practices. That is very much how I've tried to manage change within not-for-profit organisations. Really think through what business we are in, what we need to be good at, how much we should be spending on it, and benchmark it against the best.

So you would say that the measures and the challenges are similar in that respect? Do you think there has been a change since the 1990s in – I'm not saying professionalism exactly – in the not-for-profit sector, but a more results-focused, efficiency-focused approach?

Yes, I do. Absolutely. I think many, many voluntary sector organisations face tough competitive pressures in the fund-raising market and increasingly they have to meet their funding needs through short-term contracting; they are increasingly driven by those commercial pressures. I think that you have got to learn to manage those things, not to have the pressures driving you, but to actually be able to master those disciplines. So, most of the time when I have been in the voluntary sector I have been developing people so that those changes feel do-able, manageable, rather than impositions or difficulties. Because the reality is that we have all got to be in charge of those things in order to be in charge of our jobs, in order to be in charge of ourselves. And you can't deliver value and creativity in a chaotic environment. That has all got to be organised, it has got to be funded. You have got to think through in exactly the same way as the professional disciplines and be well-managed. So I have learned really very much to try to empower people through making them competent, proficient, and giving them access to the right tools.

So you would say that they are the key lessons that you have learnt throughout your whole career?

Really yes. It is about giving people the equipment to perform well, really getting them fired up, which involves their intuitive wisdom, their knowledge, their experience, their values, their beliefs ... really working on the whole person so that you have really got them engaged and they really are firing on all cylinders. And doing lots of things around – fun things – things that make them feel good about work because nobody wants to come in in the morning if they are not getting any thanks or any recognition for the job that they do. So it is about creating warmth and feeling and making people feel at home where they work and giving them quite important control over their working environment. Those sorts of things make a huge difference to how you feel about work. Same tasks – different environment.

I'm curious now. Do you think there is a difference between male and female managers in that respect? Do you think it is something that an increase in female management has brought?

I think there are still too many female managers trying to be like men. I think there is still a generation like me who still feel we should be men. A slightly half apologetic thing about it. I think increasingly this next generation coming up behind us don't have that hang-up. They are quite happy to be women. I think because of that they are doing it better, they are more relaxed and it feels more natural. There are more women of course so you don't feel quite so much under the microscope. So you are seeing a generation of women who are very used to management and feel free to flex their style. So it is more freedom to be yourself rather than to be male or female which I think is the interesting thing. I really welcome that. I think that when you get the best out of people is when they are themselves and they are not being constrained by some artificial restrictions of one kind or another. So if you can get people to be really empowered, to get on with the job, to understand what the job is and also to really use all of their talents and skills and to be natural I think it is a great way forward.

Absolutely. So, going back to the measures that you would use, say if you had been in a role for two or three years, whereas, in a commercial world you could almost measure your results, say, wholly in terms of hard cash. Would you measure the result in terms of staff retention or productivity? Do you have any sense of what the ultimate measures of good results are?

There is a wide range of measures. For example in Investors in People it was 'Who has heard of us?', 'Who is using it?' It was actually numbers. It was how many companies are registered and as it went from being a government-sponsored organisation to companies paying for it. It was my job in a way to put a value on the services we were providing and then making it a commercial proposition and also to expand the membership of Investors in People, which we did very successfully. So year on year we set ourselves growth targets, which were challenging and difficult at times. Because, you know, no one wakes up in the morning thinking 'I'm going to do "Investors in People"' and there was a lot of time, effort and organisation to achieve it. So I think those challenges of being proven in value, how you add value to the other organisation and if you think about that in a broader environment of e.g. public sector where it is a service that you are providing, how do you evaluate its benefits? It is really whether the customer comes back for more and feels well served. What does your client retention look like? How are they using the relationship – is it driving up their productivity or contributing to social well being? So it's very much that you are a provider of a service in this environment, whether you are in Social Services, whether you are in the NSPCC, whether you are working for Investors in People, or indeed whether you are working for a membership organisation as I am now.

We have all struggled with prioritising in a time-poor world. How do you balance the need for long-term planning against short-term achievement of results? Because you are constantly having to achieve and to prove your achievements. How do you balance those different priorities?

I think that's a really good question because I think particularly at the moment there's a lot of pressure on the bottom line, a lot of people are looking for that crock of gold. But for me the crock of gold can only really exist if you've got some long-term aspiration which is very, very clear and which really differentiates you from your competitors. So I think the long-term thinking needs to be very visionary, very inspirational and generally something that digs deep into the organisation and potentially then reaches out to people outside the organisation. So a set of goals and objectives which are genuinely really thought about and they don't change every five minutes but they are guiding thoughts if you like, guiding principles for the organisation. Then lots of flexibility about how you get there. Immediately people feel they are in a box they won't be creative, they won't give their best. But they are inspired if you talk to them every day about what the whole job is about and what they are there to achieve and I have found that those discussions have been fantastically rewarding in the jobs that I have done. If you really dig deep to find out why are people in this organisation, what are we here to do? It could be your stakeholder groups, your trustees, it could be your members of staff, it could be your customers, but there has to be some defining purpose. And without that sense of unity and you know ... really being all on the same side to achieve something, you can't get the cooperation in the organisation day to day that you actually need, both in the short- and long-term.

That sums up very well, doesn't it, the idea of being collaborative and giving everybody the sense that it's co-owned ...

Absolutely.

So in the organisations you have run, what has been your approach to project management? I know that's quite a broad spectrum because a project can be anything from a very small thing to the whole package?

Well, you know, organisations work hierarchically, don't they, and often in silos? And projects often run across the organisation ... they start with the product and obviously they hopefully end up in a sale, and in a service that goes on being delivered. My approach to project management is to have a clear project owner and for that project owner to be able to then tunnel through the organisation with a project team that represents all the people from the different functions. And again it is based on the ownership principle, so if you don't have a project team that represents the key elements in the project you have probably got lots of holes and people won't know what time they have to commit and probably will give it less importance compared with the day job. So you can't have hundreds of projects – probably two or three strategic projects that are running in the organisation and they need to be well led with all the inputs in place. And again you need to empower people you know, so if you have got a director team that is somewhat hierarchical then you need to empower the project managers under them to be leading on customer service or delivering value on a particular project. Maybe it is developing a product. They need to empower the people below them – the named person, the single line of accountability if you like, to actually deliver the project and recognise that that's got to be done with cross-departmental input. So to cut a long story short, good project management is about setting it up properly in the first place and getting the key people engaged and involved and probably not running too many projects, particularly if you are a small organisation as the chances are a lot of them won't get it delivered on time, they probably won't meet their budgets and essentially you are carving people up into too small slices. So keep in mind project proliferation and keep trimming it back. Review the projects. What's their purpose? Keep refreshing them. Who are they for? How are they adding to the business? What's the relationship between that project and the vision?

Which is sometimes quite hard to keep the handle on but, as you say, it's key.

It is.

Presumably you would also apply the same sort of rules to business processes generally?

Absolutely. You know I often think that we sometimes over-complicate. As I say, when you actually get down to it every business uses business processes to produce results and there will be some defining projects and processes in your business that are extremely important. And the more that you have extra projects the less time you have for those very important ones. So constantly keep an eye on the project map. Always have one person responsible for the project. So you can ring up at any time however complicated things get. You have got a dozen names on a piece of paper that define all the projects with one person who is ultimately responsible for each project. And I think if you can manage like that you are not having to progress-chase every five minutes because that person is automatically reporting in to the director team on how a particular strategic project is actually going.

In your career you have spanned, as you say, the whole spectrum really, starting with the City. Obviously for a lot of organisations their results are measured really on their customer relationships and their customer base. Can you describe the place the customer has had in the various organisations you have run?

I think the one where the customer was particularly in our sights all the time was Investors in People because the whole rationale of Investors in People was it was there as a development tool for companies and it was intended to be there as a long-term commitment from the company. There was no point in doing it and then forgetting about it. So you had to develop these long-term client relationships and continually add value and be able to demonstrate that. So if it was the Army who committed, I think, £250,000 in the first wave of commitments to Investors in People in training and development money we had to be able to validate that investment. What had it achieved? So I think that was one example, while not transactional as such, of demonstrating added value over a long period of time. And I think that gave you a really interesting insight into how to deliver customer value. And I think that was my strongest example of really delighting customers with working in Investors in People. Working with customers of all shapes and sizes. You would get a small business with no HR support and you would be talking to them about creating first of all a business plan and then a plan to develop their people and then very quickly you would establish a rapport around what this was all about and it would typically be led by the chief executive or someone reporting very close to the chief executive with no HR background at all. So you couldn't talk any of the HR gobbledy-gook. You had to talk in plain

English. And I think you know getting people to understand that this is not rocket science that managing people is actually probably the most important thing you do in business. And switching a lot of those businesses on to the Investors in People framework was a really big thing and I enjoyed it hugely.

And presumably that is a big part of your role here [CMI], and why you are here?

It is. It is getting companies and individuals to focus and develop, because if they're not they are going to get out of date. Their company, their style of management and so on can quickly lose sight of its market if the people are not being developed, if they are not thinking ahead, if they have not got the skills to perform. And I think more and more the cycle depends on being able to adapt and innovate. The technology is speeding up and people's skills have got to keep in touch with the marketplace and changes that are happening. And the price of not being in touch is that you do feel that you are struggling both as a business and as an individual.

So, do you think things are changing? Because obviously in your current role and your Investors in People role, you dealt with some big and some small organisations. Do you think there is more of an acceptance now that managing people is a big part of getting results from the organisation, because I would have said a few years ago that it wasn't perceived, particularly in bigger organisations, as relevant at all? 'Results' were the bottom line of the financial report.

I absolutely agree with that. I think there has been a change of emphasis. I still think people struggle with it not because they don't recognise it but because they don't know how to do it. And this is where competence is something we need to address very seriously. I think that if you look at the whole job of management it has become more complex. You are managing people, projects, risk, opportunity. You are managing an increasingly uncertain environment where things have a way of going pear-shaped before you've even kicked off the business plan. And you are managing lots of stakeholders. There is much more acceptance I think these days that the customer is the main stakeholder but you also have lots of people expecting things of you. So you have to be a certain strong personality and to build your skills to take that on board. I think that specifically at the CMI our challenge is to work with managers at every level, so that before you are a manager you are thinking 'These are the things I need to do, these are the competencies, these are the strengths, the resilience I need to cope with this job'. Not just to wait to fall into the pitfalls and hope you'll catch up, which is pretty much how I think management has progressed in the past. Obviously if you are a very senior manager and you've got an MBA that is a different sort of world but most of us learn management by accident. I think what we are here to do is to provide a framework of support for people which enables them to be prepared for those challenges and also to develop them through networking with other managers, opportunities to explore and look at best practice and compare notes and to really work out what is going to work for you. We all have to adapt, don't we? And use bits of the tool kit at different times. It can be a very lonely business, especially in a small company where things have changed a lot, where there is pressure on the bottom line and perhaps there is only one or two of you. So this is where I think having access to a wider group and a wider knowledge base can be fantastic. It is very liberating and I would like to see many, many more people using this resource because I think it's really valuable for them.

I think it has been very much that, particularly in the Institute's own research, it is a major failing in the UK that managers aren't supported. They are not getting the training that they want. Therefore you have to assume that an awful lot of organisations' results are affected by that.

The thing that has to be understood as well is that the employer is never going to be able to do it all. You know, there are things you can do above and beyond that as an individual. When it comes down to work you can sign up for your own learning. In a way if you can be proactive about that and not wait for your line manager to suddenly decide you need a bit of development, that's really excellent news and it can be very beneficial to your career. So if you go along to your manager and say, 'By the way, I'm learning how to be a better project manager, I'm using this module. I know how and understand how to use these spreadsheets; I'm working with other managers in other industries to actually improve my skills.' I mean that is pretty impressive. I think in this day and age we are looking for people to empower themselves.

Presumably that is going to be one of the ways you measure your own results here?

Absolutely.

I am intrigued by the vision for the Institute as a customer-focused organisation which is what we have been talking about ...

... Empowering people to help themselves, yes.
What do you see as your main steps to getting there? I know the Institute has been putting in so much work reaching out to people, building up your membership base, and your corporate membership base ...

We want to have more of a group membership base. What we aim to do is to work at corporate levels so that people feel supported by their organisation. That might be encouragement, it might be a bit of time off, it might be acknowledgement, if that's the development that people are doing. It might be that when you get to your performance review, what you review as well as the work you've been doing is the development that you've been doing with the CMI. So in other words there's greater appreciation that there are these different ways people can develop themselves and that the organisation, as well as the individual, benefits. That's what we want. For many companies this is a brilliant way of getting people switched on to learning. So we can move away from overly prescriptive managers saying you have to do this, you have to do that. It is the individual saying that no, I want to improve my skills as a manager. I am working with the Institute. These are the things I've got in place. Now, what dialogue should we be having about my ability to use and demonstrate those skills? Are there more opportunities for me to do this in the company so I can show you what I've learnt and really move my job on and take on more responsibility? So it's very much wanting to be there for people as a backstop, as a real help, a platform if you like, and a network which will help you empower your own career. I think businesses will benefit if people are more proactive in that way, and less in a way feeling that everything is about company budgets and allocating bits of training here and there. Funnily enough I think that when we have done development powered by the individual it has been stunningly successful. Look at Chartered Managers. When people that have achieved 'Chartered Manager' recount experiences they've been able to get involved with at work, projects they've been able to run, the management post they've moved into, a lot of that has been around confidence and being able to demonstrate in practice what they can do.

And that really does encompass the sort of result you're looking for at the Institute. And that brings us onto something that is really key and of interest to everybody; how your idea of getting results is obviously very people-focused.

Just to come back to how you get teams to buy into new projects, new ideas, radical change in organisations. How would you personally approach something new and get the team to buy into it?

I think it's really getting people to understand that what's happening in the world at the minute is putting more pressure on people to perform. So there are lots of real-world changes happening which mean that all of us have to deliver better results with less resources and we can only do that by working smarter. So it is continually working at the edge of what that means. And what does the CMI need to be able to offer to people that will help them work smarter? I think if you can get people to buy into that and then think well actually there are all sorts of things that we currently do that enable us. It doesn't mean reinventing the product portfolio but it might mean getting it more in front of the customer. It might mean putting more online. It might mean rethinking our approach to the marketplace, making more phone calls, instead of waiting for the customer to come to you, going to the customer, making it easy for people to access what you've got. So it often isn't what you do, it's the way that you do it. It's how far you demonstrate real customer focus by getting messages out, by getting the support network out. Going to them. Targeting different audiences. New managers typically need different things from middle managers, yet we've always had the same approach to both. So, let's look at our market then. Who is using what? And where do we think there is room for development and expansion here? It's really fine-tuning your approach and looking at what is happening in the market and then applying that knowledge and going forwards.

So it's really coming back to the customer-focus thing?

Very much. By getting people to see what we do differently. Many of our products are absolutely brilliant, but we may not say 'this is how a junior manager needs to use this'. It doesn't say this is how it's going to be used by a middle manager. It doesn't say this is how it fits into your project management if you are a senior manager. And so customising your project, making sure that we are getting it in front of people in a way that they can use it and understand it I think is a key challenge to any market. And also for people who are working out on the coal-face of membership because more and more what we see in membership organisations is the ones that are getting that offer right are doing really well. So there are always growth opportunities for organisations that are really focused in that way and have a speed of response that you don't always associate with membership organisations. You do it faster and if you do it in a dialogue and if you get people understanding that is what it's about, it's the quality of the service that you are offering which will differentiate, not just the product, then you know you are going to be really motoring ... and it's getting people focused on that and really thinking customer service. If we are going to compete and survive that is what we have to do if we are going to grow. And only one in five managers have any preparation for management in this country.

That is quite frightening, isn't it? Statistics of that kind come up all the time and it does seem to be a fundamental in the UK and elsewhere.

So there's our potential market growth you see, and therefore how we get our message out that you really could accelerate your growth as a company if you had good management skills is key. I mean nobody would get on a plane being flown by somebody who had never been trained, would they? And yet we happily put our lives in the hands of companies with a manager in charge who is learning pretty much as he or she goes along.

And not always, as we know, being supported. You referred earlier to the 'accidental manager'. I think that's very much a recognised condition, where someone is promoted to manager without the supporting training and development. Do you see any particular issues relating to this in the current climate i.e. the economic downturn?

I think the main issue in a downturn as always is that there is a temptation when things are rough and tough to not do the things where you think ... well, I don't have to do them. There is nobody standing over you making you do these things, and I think it's all too easy to cap development expenditure. Anything that looks like it's optional you are not going to do. I think in the current environment it is more important to keep your operating costs to a minimum and to keep your investment going in the things that are going to deliver the bacon, and that includes your people. Because that's the clever money. That's where the clever money is going. Otherwise we run the risk of losing our best talent and also not being able to replace it.

But the thinking does often seem to be the complete opposite, almost a short-sightedness. As you say, cost-cutting can be equated with people cutting ... or not investing in people.

It is very difficult to claw back the kind of people you want. So even if you do have to do short time for a bit, even if you do have to think about how you are going to balance the books by really cutting down on some of the non-essential costs of the business ... every business I've ever managed has had room for some cost-cutting without cutting the workforce. There are ways you can economise. So I would be looking at everything else first and trying to keep the people factor buoyant. Then ultimately, if you do have to freeze salaries, reduce hours – those sorts of things – rather than lose the skills of people that you've got.

Actually there does seem to be a bit of a trend at the moment; some of the big accountancy firms for example have tried to find alternatives to redundancy, which implies long-term investment, which is encouraging.

Yes, it is.

In your career, what would you say is the toughest challenge you've had in respect of trying to get results? Are there any particular obstacles you recall that you can talk about?

I think you know, going back to the coal industry, neither side were going to agree and it didn't matter how clever we were about the wording of different agreements and so on, we were on a collision course. I think sometimes, with the best will in the world people are determined to fall out and an awful lot of resource gets wasted that way. I just think these days, you know, we do tend to go about problem-solving in a more intelligent way. There are fewer of those deadlocked positions, and I think for my money it is much more about really focusing on the areas where management and the workforce can cooperate. Given that we are all here to try to maximise the combined welfare and trying to keep people in jobs, trying to keep businesses going ... I mean, really getting down to it, not talking in theory, but getting down to the specific issues and getting on with it. I think people are quite impatient with a lot of waffle that goes on about the importance of skills and training. Let's get down to it. You know, we've heard the hype. We know it all. The issue is how do we deliver it? How do we enhance the skills of people so they stay in jobs, they are not on the scrapheap, they don't then have to be retrained when they come back into the workforce because they have stayed in the workforce. They are being flexible. They are being adaptable, and they are moving on. If you can keep businesses and people agile, toned up, ready to move, healthy – those are the things that I think will stand us in really good stead.

Earlier you mentioned the deadlock situation with the coal industry. How personally do you deal with frustrations? Do you literally bang your head against a wall or do you walk around a corner and swear a bit and come back or ...

I think we all have to count to ten sometimes ... because the trouble is, you can make an enemy in an instant and it takes years to make a real friend of a colleague at work. It's very valuable and you need their cooperation. Sometimes you know things don't look good. People say or do things which they don't necessarily mean. So I think you have to bite your tongue, and try to make a mature judgement. Try to get through the difficulties you might be having and I think ... above and beyond that I think always surround yourself with the right people so that between them you will have all the strengths of the team. They won't all be brilliant at everything, but if you've got a team where you've got a good thinker, a good doer, a good creator, yes, and you have got those complementary skills around you, if you just ask the right questions you will get the answers to the problems that you are getting. Between you, you may not see the answer yourself, it doesn't actually matter. I used to think that being a leader you have to fix the lot but you don't, that's the reason why you have a team! You are not there to fix the lot. So if you are stuck, and things are feeling a bit grim say well, I think things are a bit grim, and I'm worrying about these three problems. Just the exercise of saying what the three problems are gets it off your chest. And then, take on board what people are saying and listen. Because if you've got a good team around you the chances are they will see a way forward between you. And I think once you get locked into this, you know, the management think this and the unions think that, there's no way forward, because they are determined to fall out. So try to get a wider discussion going and really get some of the solutions on the table. When we have our meetings now, when a director, for example, comes up with an issue, a problem, I always ask them first of all, 'well, what would your suggested solution be?' So even if they don't know it makes them think OK, so what are the options here? Then other people chip in with other options and before you know where you are you have moved it from a problem to perhaps three things you could do about it. So it's again about getting people to think solutions as well as problems.

And again, that's moving away from perhaps the old-fashioned dictatorial method of management to the collaborative one.

And usually if it's their idea it becomes much more powerful than if it's your idea. I know I totally didn't understand that when I first started being chief executive, that actually if someone has just said something and they seem to be getting a hold of the situation and it looks like a good idea and they fundamentally have the line accountability for it, it's much more important for you to back that idea than to come up with some rival idea of your own.

Do you have ways of dealing with team stresses and pressures, perhaps where a situation or project has become gridlocked?

Yes, sometimes it helps to keep it light, do your away-days, have fun. You know, I find sometimes just by getting away from the problem, you come back to it the next day and actually it doesn't look such a big problem.

So, when things have got stuck, the brakes have got locked on ... it moves it forward?

And having fun at work is essential. You know, we try regularly to have days with staff when we do a sports day or we do a fund-raising day, we do something like that. Twice a year, perhaps even three times a year, we have a regular event of some kind. And again, it isn't always the same thing and the ideas for these events come from the staff themselves and I think that is a great way of getting the whole company together to have fun. And people start to say OK, instead of questioning or giving your task to someone else you start to see that it's a personal interaction you need to have and you start eating away at some of the silos that can develop and you start developing proper teams across the organisation as well. And that has all come out of having a fun time together.

Do you think that scenario is being adopted universally, and particularly again in this climate where everybody is so frightened of incurring non-essential costs? For instance many organisations seem to be cutting, say, their Christmas party and I wonder if, while people accept that they may not get

a pay rise, sometimes that Christmas party can mean more to them ... it can feel like the final slap in the face sometimes, can't it?

Yes, well we didn't have a pay rise this year but we have kept going with these events and I think the point of these events is that they are such a worthwhile investment. They cost time and we run them ourselves. But people feel very strongly about this team thing and because that's getting embedded now if we were to suddenly say all right, we are never going to have any more of these things going on I think it would be such a negative signal. It's not that we were ever flashing lots of cash you know, it was always about people putting the time in. And of course, that time could be spent on the customer but I think if you look after your staff they will look after the customers.

That seems fundamental and I think that is something we very much want to bring out in all of the books in this series because obviously we are promoting all of the management standards.

It sounds like you have got exciting times ahead here at the CMI?

It is exciting. We have got some great people in the CMI and also a lot of knowledge. I am absolutely convinced we have got a first rate offer and, as I say, with the emphasis more on asking 'How do we put this in front of the customer?', 'How do we engage with the customer?' and taking that extra time and trouble, I think we've got a great future, plus the fact that there are all those managers out there who basically need what we've got. It's a big marketplace and we've got lots and lots of things to offer them, the membership, new members coming in, young members coming in, they love the CMI. Again, I think that's a really good point you know because they see the point in having professional skills, which perhaps their parents didn't. Older managers in the workforce have probably not understood so much. They have not had so much investment themselves. They now understand about qualifications, they understand about getting a degree, they understand about the role of study, and of analysis. They understand about the getting of skills, etc. So I think we can build a new generation of managers who set higher expectations for themselves and who want a little more as a result.

You must be really excited actually about the re-launch as another big push forward to getting the results that you want?

We want to be noticed out there and that is what the rebranding is about. The brand does look good and I think it will be recognisable. But I think it is important for the people here to know what the brand stands for, what our values are and what we believe in. And that's all of them putting the products in the shop window, customising the product and working out who wants what and making sure that we don't hang back, because this is a marketplace where we need to go out there and sell what we do.

Managing customer needs checklist

If you are thinking about how better to manage your customers' needs, here are some issues to think about. You might want to find a few, valuable minutes to take a clean sheet of paper and jot down any ideas that the following list generates.

Market and customer research
What are you doing differently, or better, than your competitors? What could you be doing even better? Do your sales skills need a makeover? What mechanisms do you have in place for 'spotting a gap in the market and a market in the gap'?

Consumer testing
How often do you talk to your customers about what they like, and don't like, about your products and services? Do you listen to what they say? What action have you taken as a result? Can you honestly say that you 'never, ever go forward without checking it with the consumer'?

Knowing who your customers are
How well can you define who your customers actually are? Are your customers different from the end users of your product? Who do you market and sell to? What measures are in place to communicate with both groups? Do you have a long-term 'game plan' and are your customers part of it?

(Continued)

(Continued)

Credibility gap

Are you passionate about what you do? Does this come across to those around you? Are you confident in your products and services? Do you believe in them? Do people have confidence in you?

Getting close to your customers

Are your team members and colleagues ambassadors for your organisation? Would you feel confident if they met and spoke with your customers? Have you assembled the best possible team that you could? As your organisation grows, are you still as close to your customers as you once were?

Innovation

Can you think of examples where you have deliberately gone 'against the grain'? Do you struggle with the concept that you are meeting your customers' needs, but that they may not know what their needs are? Can you and do you 'zig' when those around you 'zag'?

Determination

Are you tempted to give up? Do you tend to see things through? Where are you on your journey?

National Occupational Standards

This book covers the NOS Management and Leadership standard – Achieving Results (as at 2008). The following table will help you to locate these competencies in the book.

Competency	Unit	Chapter number	Chapter title
Manage a project	F1	2	How can you manage projects and processes to get results?
Manage a programme of complementary projects	F2	2	How can you manage projects and processes to get results?
Manage business processes	F3	2	How can you manage projects and processes to get results?

Competency	Unit	Chapter number	Chapter title
Develop and review a framework for marketing	F4	3	Who are your customers?
Resolve customer service problems	F5	5	Do you have customer service problems?
Monitor and resolve customer service problems	F6	5	Do you have customer service problems?
Support customer service improvements	F7	6	How can you improve customer service?
Work with others to improve customer service	F8	6	How can you improve customer service?
Build your organisation's understanding of its market and customers	F9	3	Who are your customers?
Develop a customer-focused organisation	F10	4	Why is good customer service important?
Managing the achievement of customer satisfaction	F11	7	How can you be sure customers are satisfied?
Improve organisational performance	F12	11	How can you improve performance in your organisation?

Competency	Unit	Chapter number	Chapter title
Manage quality systems	F13	8	Why does quality matter?
Prepare for and participate in quality audits	F14	8	Why does quality matter?
Carry out quality audits	F15	8	Why does quality matter?
Manage the development and marketing of products/services in your area of responsibility	F16	9	Have you got the right product or service?
Manage the delivery of customer service in your area of responsibility	F17	7	How can you be sure customers are satisfied?
Prepare sales proposals and deliver sales presentations	F18	10	What does it take to generate sales?
Sell products/services to customers	F19	10	What does it take to generate sales?

Further information and reading

Useful organisations and websites

Chartered Management Institute
Management House
Cottingham Road
Corby NN17 1TT
tel 01536 204222
www.managers.co.uk
For information about all aspects of management and management qualifications.

Management Standards centre
3rd Floor, 2 Savoy Court
Strand
London WC2R 0EZ
tel 020 7240 2826
www.management-standards.org.home

Department for Business, Innovations and Skills
Ministerial Correspondence Unit
1 Victoria St
London SW1H 0EY
tel 0207 215 5000
www.berr.gov.uk
For information about all aspects of business including benchmarking and innovation.

Official UK Government website
www.direct.gov.uk
For a wide variety of information including employment and education.

Office of Fair Trading
www.oft.gov.uk
For information on legislation affecting businesses.

Institute of Chartered Accountants in England and Wales
www.icaew.co.uk
For information about KPIs.

Chartered Institute of Marketing
www.cim.co.uk
For information on marketing, customer service and using KPIs.

Marketing UK
www.marketinguk.co.uk
For information about market reports.

BSI British Standards
tel 020 8996 9001

Business Link
tel 0845 600 9006
www.businesslink.gov.uk
Business Link is a government-funded network of local advice centres for business.

Chambers of Commerce
www.chamberonline.co.uk
Local Chambers of Commerce are good sources of information on a variety of local and national business matters.

Investors in People
helpline 0207 467 1946
www.investorsinpeople.co.uk

Microsoft Small Business Centre
www.microsoft.com/uk/smallbusiness
For information about software that will help with collecting and analysing customer information.

Design Council
www.designcouncil.org.uk
For information about product design and innovation.

British Retail Consortium
www.brc.org.uk
For information about retail selling.

Institute of Business Consulting
helpline 0207 566 5220

Learndirect
www.learndirect-business.com
For advice about all sorts of business training and courses.

Market Research Society
www.mrs.org.uk
For information about market research.

Research Buyer's Guide
www.rbg.org.uk
For information about market research agencies.

Engineering Construction Industry Training Board (ECITB)
www.ecitb.org.uk
tel 01923 260 000

Association for Project Management (APM)
www.apm.org.uk
tel 0845 458 1944

Small Firms Enterprise and Development Initiative
www.sfedi.co.uk
tel 0114 241 2155

Institute of Customer Service
www.instituteofcustomerservice.com
tel 01206 571 716

Linked In
www.linkedin.com
A professional network of contacts.

Useful reading

Adair, John, *Decision Making and Problem Solving* (CIPD) 1999
Baguley, Phil, *Performance Management in a Week* (Hodder & Stoughton) 2002

Baguley, Phil, *Teach Yourself Project Management* (Teach Yourself) 2008

Barker, Stephen and Cole, Rob, *Brilliant Project Management: What the Best Project Managers Know, Say and Do* (Prentice Hall) 2007

Bird, Polly *Teach Yourself Time Management* (Teach Yourself) 2008

Cook, Sarah, *Customer Care Excellence: Create an Effective Customer Service Strategy* (Kogan Page) 2002

Gitomer, Jeffrey, *The Sales Bible: The Ultimate Sales Resource* (John Wiley & Sons) 2003

Kemp, Sid, *Quality Management Demystified* (McGraw-Hill) 2006

Oppenhaiem, A., *Questionnaire Design, Interviewing and Attitude Measurement* (Pinter) 1992

Peppit, Ed, *Six of the Best – Lessons in Life and Leadership* (Hodder Arnold) 2007

Portny, Stanley E., *Project Management for Dummies* (John Wiley & Sons) 2006

Walmsley, Bernice, *Teach Yourself Training* (Teach Yourself) 2005

And other titles in the Instant Manager series.

Index